YOUR BLUEPRINT
FOR FINANCIAL LITERACY

Your Blueprint for Financial Literacy

A Better Understanding of
Personal Finances Regardless of Age

Salzman Epstein Tarver

THE FINANCIAL COMPASS
Guiding you to financial literacy

Your Blueprint for Financial Literacy:
A Better Understanding of Personal Finances Regardless of Age

This book was developed using the author's original research, experience, and analysis. Select AI-based tools were used in a limited, supportive role during research and revision, including summarizing publicly available information and reviewing grammar and clarity. All content, interpretations, and final decisions are the author's own, and the author is fully responsible for the accuracy and viewpoints expressed in this work.

Figures, examples, and projections in this book are for illustrative and educational purposes only and may vary based on real-world conditions and individual circumstances

Printed in the United States of America

Salzman Epstein Tarver
Financial Compass Publishing

THE FINANCIAL COMPASS

Bronx, NY
YourFinancialLiteracyBlueprint.com

LCCN: 2025922329
ISBN: 979-8-9935215-0-3

For everyone who didn't have the guidance to navigate personal finance—may this book be your compass to clarity, confidence, and independence.

For Aunt Little Bit, whose wisdom, warmth, and faith taught me that generosity and discipline are the true foundations of wealth.

And for the children of Little Flower—and every young person who dares to build a brighter future despite the odds—may knowledge light your path and hope guide your future.

Contents

PREFACE

When I was a child, there was a course in high school called home economics. In that course, students would learn what were considered essential skills needed to properly run and maintain a household. Sewing and cooking were among the core subjects. Girls took the course to become better cooks and learn to sew. Boys usually took the course to meet girls and rarely learned how to sew or cook. I later thought of the term *economics* as relating to finances. I never understood why the course was called home economics until later in life. I eventually realized that some essential financial topics were missing, creating major gaps in personal financial awareness. I thought writing this book would be a great way to help the students of life's personal finances close such essential knowledge gaps by offering a blueprint that simplifies complex financial topics. After a bit of research on the subject, I have listed some eye-opening findings of a study conducted by MarketWatch in 2024:[1]

- Only 57% of adults in the United States are financially literate.
- Missouri, Utah, and Virginia boast the best financial literacy rates, while Alaska, Washington, DC, and South Dakota have the worst.
- Over 40% of adults in the United States are unfamiliar

1 Clara Haverstic, "Financial Illiteracy and Its Impact on Your Wallet," MarketWatch Guides, March 28, 2025, https://www.marketwatch.com/financial-guides/banking/financial-literacy-statistics/.

with Roth IRAs, money market accounts, and high-yield savings accounts, but nearly 70% of adults in the United States who are familiar with 401(k)s don't use them.

- Older generations tend to be more financially literate. Baby boomers are the most likely to be familiar with saving and investment products like 401(k) and Roth IRA retirement accounts, money market accounts, and CDs. At the same time, more than half of Generation Z members were unfamiliar with CDs, high-yield money market accounts, or Roth IRAs.
- The average US citizen scores 46% on a basic quiz about financial literacy, showcasing a critical gap in financial education.
- Only 29% of US citizens in the survey reported taking a personal finance course in high school. In general, those who took a course report greater familiarity with financial tools and products.

Many phases in life relate to finance and living responsibilities, and looking at these statistics and others, I created this blueprint and compass to help guide you down each road and combine the most critical information in one convenient place. This information can be found in many sources—Investopedia, SmartAsset, and government and banking websites—but it's scattered. I've compiled it into a one-stop reference. This book will assist you in curbing some of life's confusions about financial and living responsibilities that have plagued me and many others.

I've had small and odd jobs to earn money from as early as the age of twelve. I took on my first real paying job at Big Bear Super Foods while in high school as a bagger, floor mopper, trash emptier, stock boy, and escort to people who needed help getting their groceries to their cars. I started to learn the real value and understanding of saving money and the truth that money indeed does not grow on trees. All of my earnings, except for twenty dollars per week that I kept as spending money, went to my Aunt Little Bit, with whom I lived during the final two years of my high school career. She kept my earnings in a place unknown to anyone, except for herself and Uncle Russell, and she only issued funds out to me when I could show a solid need for it, backed up by undeniable evidence and proof. I didn't have a bank account. She served as both the bank teller and the branch manager. Truth be told, I'd only ever entered a bank with my mother as a child or as a teenager to ask if they had any summer jobs I could do. The answer was always no.

There is an old saying, "If I knew then what I know now." As I reflect on those earlier times, I often find myself repeating those words to myself. I've learned that home economics is much more than sewing and cooking. Whether you are a teenager, a young adult, a young veteran converting to civilian life, an immigrant newly arriving in the United States, or an adult in general, some subjects and responsibilities are unavoidable when it comes to personal finances. Life has many financial phases, and they appear whether you're ready or not.

Not being armed with this essential knowledge can often lead to headaches and playing catch-up later in life. Having a true understanding of these crucial areas in personal finance can determine whether you get the best interest rates available when buying a car or a home. It can determine whether you'll be able to make your money work for you and in your best interest and whether you'll be ready to retire when you're no longer able to work. Knowledge of these essential life subjects can influence whether you'll live paycheck to paycheck and barely get by. Some areas in this book cover subjects that some people never understand, although they are affected by them. This book will serve as an opportunity for you to get ahead of those responsibilities before they surface, or even if they've already shown up uninvited.

My experience has shown me that an event is only an opportunity if you're aware that it's an opportunity. If you are unaware of its significance, you won't be able to take advantage of it. Being armed with knowledge from this quick guide to personal finances will enable you to see opportunities when they surface; it'll also enable you to create opportunities that wouldn't otherwise exist. This book doesn't teach you how to invest in the stock market or which insurance is better. I wrote it to give you a better understanding of essential financial information when it's time to play the game of life and become more independent. Knowing this information will get you started further down the field. Many of us start deep in our end zones when we are trying to score in the game of life's personal finances. As you tackle each chapter, you'll find a few recurring topics, issues, or terms. However, you'll soon learn how each subject connects and how one can affect another.

Source: Your Blueprint for Financial Literacy

Chapter 1

What Are Checking and Savings Accounts, and Do I Need One?

Before we define checking and savings accounts, let's begin with what a bank is. You might be thinking, "Who doesn't know what a bank is?" Well, don't get ahead of yourself. According to Merriam-Webster.com, *bank* (noun) can be defined as the following:[2]

1. "The land alongside or sloping to a river or lake"
2. "A slope, mass, or mound of a particular substance (e.g., a snowbank)"

For the purposes of this book, *bank* is defined as a federal institution licensed to receive deposits and make loans. We'll focus on banks as they relate to personal finance. There are several types of banks including retail, commercial or corporate, investment, and central. Let's discuss and become more familiar with each of them. Below is a list of banks as defined by Investopedia:[3]

Retail bank. Retail banks serve individual customers and are commonly found along busy town centers and main streets for easy access. These institutions offer a wide range of personal financial

2 "Bank," *Merriam-Webster.com Dictionary*, Merriam-Webster, last modified August 17, 2025, https://www.merriam-webster.com/dictionary/bank.

3 Adam Barone, "How Banking Works, Types of Banks, and How to Choose the Best Bank for You," Investopedia, March 28, 2023, https://www.investopedia.com/terms/b/bank.asp.

services, including checking and savings accounts, auto loans, mortgages, personal loans, and credit cards such as MasterCard and Visa. We'll focus primarily on this type of bank—its services, how it supports everyday financial needs, and its role in home economics and personal finance. Some of the most well-known retail banks include Bank of America, Citibank, Capital One, and Chase Bank (JPMorgan Chase).

Commercial or corporate bank. Some banks focus on helping businesses, from small companies to large corporations. They offer services like lending to businesses, managing cash flow, financing commercial properties, handling employee payroll, and facilitating trade and international business. Big banks like JPMorgan Chase and Bank of America are some examples. Even though they work with businesses, many also have branches that serve individuals.

Investment bank. Some banks specialize in serving business clients, ranging from small companies to large corporations. These institutions typically offer services such as business credit lines, cash flow management, commercial property financing, payroll solutions, and support for domestic and international trade. Well-known examples include JPMorgan Chase (Investment division of JPMorgan Chase), Bank of America Merrill Lynch, Morgan Stanley, and Barclays Capital. Although their primary focus may be on commercial banking, many also offer personal banking services through separate retail divisions.

Central bank. I actually worked at one of these types of banks at one point. As an individual customer, you won't go to them for checking or savings accounts, but they play a powerful role in your everyday financial life. These banks help keep the country's money stable, control inflation, set interest rates, and manage how much money is in circulation. In the US, this type of bank is called the **Federal Reserve** bank. It might sound like just one big bank, but it's spread out across different cities, including Boston, New York, Philadelphia, Cleveland, Richmond, Atlanta, Chicago, St. Louis, Minneapolis, Kansas City, Dallas, and San Francisco. I worked for the New York branch, but the location I worked at was located in East Rutherford, New Jersey.

Now that we know the types of banks that exist, we can determine which ones will be of most interest to us in our personal finances. The question asked was *What are savings and checking accounts?* Savings and checking accounts are very important in home economics and personal finance, and whether you're learning at home, in school, or as an adult with growing responsibilities, you'll see why. Did you know you can open a checking account as early as age thirteen? As my Aunt Little Bit used to say, "Now, ain't that something for your money!" The catch to this is that usually a parent or guardian is required to be a joint owner until you turn eighteen. However, at age thirteen, you can monitor and access this account if you wish to. Now that you understand what a bank is, you can go into one with a guardian and find out how to open an account, or you can open one for your children. Finally, somewhere to put your lemonade stand and birthday money!

The checking account is a deposit account held at a financial institution that lets you deposit and withdraw money as needed. Once you open a checking account, you can access it in several ways: by writing checks, using automated teller machines (ATMs), or making electronic payments through debit cards or online banking.

What makes checking accounts different from other accounts, like savings, is that they usually allow unlimited deposits and frequent withdrawals. Savings accounts, however, often limit how many times you can take money out. There are a few key things to know about how checking accounts work.

- Most checking accounts don't earn much interest—if they offer any at all.
- You can add money to your account in several ways, including using an ATM, setting up direct deposit from

your employer, or transferring funds electronically with mobile apps, checks, or debit and credit cards that are linked to your account.

- Be aware of the fees tied to certain checking accounts. For example, you might get charged for spending more than what's in your account (an **overdraft**), for writing too many checks, or even for letting your balance fall below a set minimum. I remember having a checking account that charged me a fee anytime my balance dropped below $1,000. To understand what your options are, it's best to talk to your bank and ask about the features they offer.

Q&A SESSION

What's the Difference Between Checking and Savings Accounts?

A checking account is mainly used for everyday spending, while a savings account is designed to help you set money aside and earn interest over time. When you put money into a savings account and leave it there, the bank rewards you by paying interest, helping your balance grow. Some savings accounts offer better interest rates than others, so comparing your options is worth the effort.

Checking accounts come with features that make managing your daily finances easy. For example, banks give you a **debit card** you can use to deposit or withdraw money and to make purchases—whether it's buying a gift, going to a sports event, or eating out. You'll also receive paper checks, known as a **checkbook**, and you can have things like wages or transfers from other accounts directly deposited. Most checking accounts include overdraft protection, which we talked about earlier. You can use a debit card at ATMs, not just from your bank but often at other banks and store locations as well. You'll also have access to online and mobile banking, where you can pay bills, move money between accounts, and set up alerts for deposits or withdrawals.

Unlike savings accounts, checking accounts usually don't earn much—or any—interest. Banks offer interest on savings accounts using what's called annual percentage yield (APY). This is the percentage you earn on your savings, including the effect of **compound interest** throughout the year. That means as your interest is added to your account, it starts earning more interest, and your balance slowly grows over time. The more you save, the more you stand to earn. Some banks base their interest rates on rates set by the Federal Reserve bank.

It's important not to confuse APY (annual percentage yield) with APR (annual percentage rate). APY is used to show how much interest you *earn* on your savings, while APR shows how much interest you'll *pay* when you borrow money. APY includes the effects of compounding, but APR does not. We'll talk more about APR and APY later in chapter 3.

Why Do I Need to Open a Savings and Checking Account?

In the United States—and as I discovered while living in the United Kingdom, as well as in many other developed and developing countries—it's extremely difficult to conduct business transactions without a checking account. While there's no single official statistic, combining the data suggests that roughly 80%–90% of jobs require or strongly encourage having a checking account.[4] This is the preferred way companies pay your wages. The bank you've opened a checking account with will issue you checks, but you may find it more beneficial to pay bills electronically. You'll be able to make purchases or ATM withdrawals using a linked debit card without having to go into the bank to withdraw money.

If you've ever heard of saving for a rainy day, you'll definitely find savings accounts useful. Remember, unlike the checking account, the savings account is a deposit account that's designed

4 Payroll Partners, "Can You Make Direct Deposit Mandatory?," Payroll Partners, accessed April 10, 2025, https://www.payrollpartners.com/make-direct-deposit-mandatory/.

to hold money that isn't for everyday use. I've opened a savings account as a safety net for hard times, like job losses or car repairs or plumbing and other home issues. This account is usually for putting money away to save for large purchases, like big trips, a new car, or a home—not your daily expenses.

What's a Check, and What Do All Those Numbers Mean at the Bottom of a Check?

"A **check** is a physical document used to tell a bank to transfer a specific amount of money from one account to another."[5] The person or business writing the check is called the **payor**, and the one receiving the money is the **payee**. The bank that handles the transaction is referred to as the **drawee**. There are several types of checks, such as certified, cashier's, and payroll—also known as paychecks.

Checks can be used to either deposit money into a bank account or to withdraw it as cash. When a check is processed, the bank removes the funds from the payor's account, usually from checking but sometimes savings or another account type. The check serves as a formal instruction to the bank to move money from the person issuing it to the person named on the check.

Standard features of a check include the date it was written, the payee's name, the payment amount, the signature of the account holder, and a memo line for notes. Along the bottom of the check, you'll see a line of numbers printed in magnetic ink. These numbers are called the magnetic ink character recognition (**MICR**) strip and sit just beneath the memo and signature lines. The MICR strip typically includes the bank's routing number, the account number, and the individual check number. In the next section, we'll take a closer look at these numbers, and I'll explain what each one means.

5 Julia Kagan, "Check: What It Is, How Bank Checks Work, and How to Write One," Investopedia, May 29, 2024, https://www.investopedia.com/terms/c/check.asp.

How Do I Write a Check?

Not all checks look exactly alike, but most include the same important parts. In the top-left corner, you'll usually find the name and contact details of the person who wrote the check. The name of the bank where the person's account is held also appears somewhere on the check, often in the middle. Several sections on the check must be completed by the person writing it:[6]

- The **date line** is where you write the date the check is being issued. It's usually found in the upper right-hand corner.
- The **payee line** says *Pay to the Order of* and is where you write the name of the person or business you are paying.
- The **amount box** is a small box, usually to the right of the payee line, where you write the amount of money in numbers—for example, $150.00.
- The **amount in words line** is below the payee line; it's a long line where you write out the amount in words—for example, one hundred-fifty dollars and zero cents. This helps prevent fraud and confirms the number written in the box.
- The **memo line** is found in the bottom-left corner; this section lets you write a short note about what the check is for—like rent or a gift. This part is optional but helpful.
- The **signature line** is where the account holder signs the check. Without a signature, the check isn't valid and the bank can't process it.
- The **check number, routing number, and account number** are the series of numbers along the bottom edge of the check. The first is the bank's routing number,

6 Kagan, "Check: What It Is."

which identifies the bank. The second is the account number, and the third is the check number.

Only federally chartered and state-chartered banks that are eligible to maintain an account at the Federal Reserve bank are issued **routing transit numbers**. Routing transit numbers are often used when setting up a wire transfer or direct deposit. This will be useful when you need to set up direct deposit or if you want to set up autopay for bills such as cable television, credit card bills, etc. Figure 1.1 shows an example:

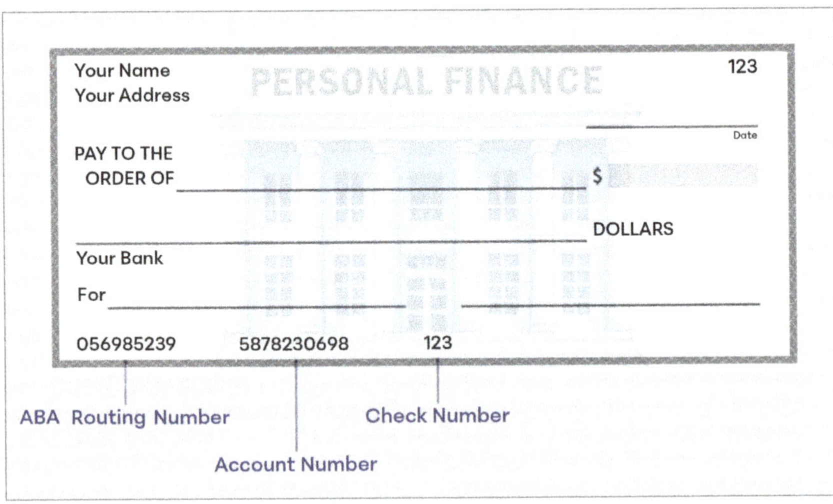

Figure 1.1 Source: Your Blueprint for Financial Literacy

Why Do People Sign the Back of a Check?

When someone gives you a check as payment, you'll usually need to sign the back of it before you can deposit or cash it. This process is called **endorsing a check**. Endorsement is required so the bank or financial institution can release the money to the right person.

It's a simple step but an important one that also helps protect you from fraud. There are different ways to endorse a check depending on the situation, but most involve signing your name on the back to show you are the rightful recipient. Knowing how to endorse a check is a key part of financial literacy, and there are a few common types of endorsements:[7]

Restrictive endorsement. To use a restrictive endorsement, write ***For deposit only*** on the back of the check. Under that, write your account number, then sign your name on the next line. This tells the bank the check is only meant to be deposited into your account, which adds some security. But there's a small risk—if the person who gave you the check gets a copy of it through their bank, they might see your account number. If you have privacy concerns, you can just write *For deposit only* and skip the account number. This is still okay, but it's a little less secure than writing all three lines.

Endorsing a check to a third party. You can use a check that was written to you to pay someone else instead. This is called a **special endorsement**, and it transfers the money from the check to another person. To do this, go to the endorsement area at the back of the check, then follow these steps:

1. Write *Pay to the order of*, followed by the name of the person you want to give the money to.
2. Sign your *own name* directly underneath.

The person you're giving the check to will then need to sign their name below yours before they can deposit or cash it. Keep in mind, this isn't the most secure way to send money. Some banks won't accept this kind of endorsement unless both people are there in person with ID. In many cases, the bank may require you to deposit

7 Kiara Taylor, "How to Endorse a Check," Investopedia, July 2, 2024, https://www.Investopedia.com/how-to-endorse-a-check-5188585.

the check into your own account first, then send the money using another method. If you still want to use this method, make sure that *both banks* involved—the one that issued the check and the one receiving it—will accept this type of endorsement. If they don't, the check may be rejected, and the funds won't go through.

Blank endorsement. This type of endorsement is the *least secure*, but blank endorsements are also the most common. With this method, you simply sign your name on the back of the check. Then, you tell the bank teller whether you want to deposit it into an account or cash it. You can also use this type of endorsement when depositing a check using an ATM or mobile banking. Even though it's not very secure, you can reduce the risk of someone else using your check by waiting to sign it until *right before* depositing it.

Business endorsement. Sometimes, a check is written out to a business instead of a person. When that happens, the check must be signed on behalf of the business by someone who is authorized to do so. This kind of endorsement is a little more detailed, but it's still done in the same spot on the back of the check where personal endorsements go. To endorse a check made out to a business, follow these steps:

1. Write the name of the business on the first line.
2. On the line below, sign your name and print your job title clearly.

Mobile endorsement. If you're like me and many others, you probably use your bank's mobile app or website to deposit checks. When using this method, your bank may ask you to endorse the check in a certain way. Some banks require you to write *For mobile deposit only* under your signature to accept the check. Since not all banks have the same rules, it's a good idea to check your bank's guidelines before depositing a check this way. Figure 1.2 is a sample illustration showing what each of the endorsement types looks like.

In the illustration that follows, you'll see the names of my nieces, Sophia and Crissi. I'm using them here as examples to show how different check endorsements look in real life.

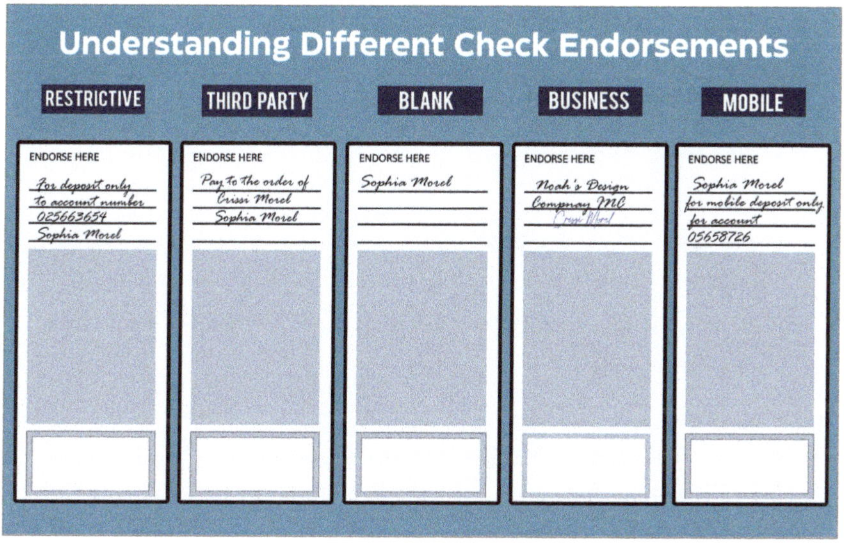

Figure 1.2 Source: Your Blueprint for Financial Literacy

How Do I Deposit Money into the Bank?

Now that you have access to money, you may want to keep it safe by depositing it in a bank. You can deposit money into different types of accounts, such as savings, checking, or money market accounts. As the account holder, you have the right to take out or deposit money, based on the terms you agreed to when you opened the account.

Both savings and checking accounts can receive deposits. Even though the bank holds your money, it still belongs to you. You can take it out anytime, transfer it to someone else, or use it to make purchases. In many cases, banks require you to make a **minimum deposit** to open a new account. When you deposit money into a savings or interest-earning account, the bank pays you **interest**, a small percentage added to your account at regular times.

The amount of interest you earn depends on the bank's rate and how often the interest is added or compounded. There are two main types of deposits: demand deposits and time deposits.[8]

- A **demand deposit** is a regular bank account—like a checking or savings account—where you can take out your money at any time.
- The **time deposit** requires you to keep your money in the account for a set amount of time. A common example is a certificate of deposit (CD), which usually pays a higher interest rate than a regular savings account. But in exchange, you agree not to withdraw the money until the term ends.

How Do I Withdraw Money from the Bank?

You can withdraw your money from a bank in several ways.[9]

Use an ATM. If you have an **ATM card** or debit card connected to your bank account, you can use an ATM (automated teller machine) to take out cash when you need it. While these machines may look a little different, most work the same way. You insert your card, enter your **PIN** (personal identification number), choose the account you want to use, type in the amount you want to withdraw, and wait for your cash and a printed receipt. Keep in mind that most ATMs only dispense certain bills, like tens or twenties. There may also be limits on how much you can withdraw at one time or in a single day.

If you use your bank's ATM, there's usually no fee. But if you use an ATM that belongs to another bank or company, you may be charged a fee. Some banks refund these fees if you're a preferred

8 Julia Kagan, "Deposit: Definition, Meaning, Types, and Example," Investopedia, December 14, 2023, https://www.investopedia.com/terms/d/deposit.asp.

9 FBNO, "How to Withdraw Money from Your Bank Account," May 18, 2021, https://www.fnbo.com/insights/2021/personal-finance/how-to-withdraw-money-bank-account.

customer, but not all do. Always remember to take your card before leaving the machine to protect yourself from fraud. To avoid extra fees, I sometimes ask for **cash back** when I make purchases at the grocery store. This lets you get cash without using an ATM, and there's usually no fee for doing it.

Write a check. If you have a checking, money market, or another type of account that allows checks, you can write a check to withdraw money. To do this, simply fill in the cash amount on the check and take it to your bank. Present the check to the teller along with a valid form of identification. If you have enough funds in your account, the teller will give you the amount of cash written on the check. Just be careful when writing checks, especially if you are giving them to someone else or carrying them with you. If a check is lost or stolen, and it's already signed, someone else might try to use it. Some banks have made the check-cashing process even easier—rather than writing a check, you can insert your ATM or debit card into a card reader at the teller window, enter your PIN, and get your money without needing a written form.

Fill out a withdrawal slip. If you don't have checks linked to your account, you can still take out money by visiting your bank in person and filling out a **withdrawal slip**. Start by writing the date, the name on the account, and your account number. If you don't know your account number, the teller can look it up using your ID and debit card. Next, write the amount you want to withdraw. If you're not sure how to fill it out, a teller or banker at your branch can guide you through the process.

Link your account to a peer-to-peer payment service. The world becomes more digital every day, and that includes the way we send and receive money. Another way to access the cash in your bank account is by connecting it to a **peer-to-peer (P2P) payment app**, such as Venmo, Zelle, or PayPal. These apps are a popular way to pay for small purchases. Just make sure to use these services only with people you know and trust. Use a PIN or password to keep your account secure, set your profile to private, and turn on notifications to stay updated on account activity. If you're unsure how to adjust these settings, your bank can help you set everything up.

How Do Interest Rates Apply to My Savings and Checking Accounts?

Retail banks decide the interest rates they offer on savings accounts, but those rates are influenced by the overall economy. At the most basic level, a bank's savings interest rate depends on two things: (1) how much the bank wants people to deposit money and (2) how much customers value having a safe place to store their savings. These factors are also affected by central banks and government policies, which help guide interest rates across the entire economy.[10] You may remember that we talked about central banks earlier—this is one of the ways they influence how money moves.

Supply and demand apply to savings accounts. Most savings accounts are considered **liquid**, which means you can access your money easily, and your original balance—also known as the **principal**—is protected. Many people like savings accounts because they are both safe and flexible. Banks offer savings accounts to attract deposits from customers. They use that money to fund loans for other customers. When banks need more cash, they might raise interest rates on savings accounts to encourage people to deposit money. If they want to slow down how much is going out, they may lower those rates. Banks have to be careful not to offer more interest than they can make from loans or other investments—otherwise, they won't earn a profit. People who have extra money to save often compare the interest rates on savings accounts with other options like bonds, certificates of deposit (CDs), or money market accounts. Each of these savings tools comes with its own level of risk, return, and accessibility.

10 Sean Ross, "How Savings Account Interest Rates Are Determined," Investopedia. October 29, 2023, https://www.investopedia.com/ask/answers/043015/what-economic-factors-affect-savings-account-rates.asp.

Everyone has different preferences, and it's all about finding the right balance between security and earning potential. I prefer using a **high-yield savings account** because I can withdraw my money at any time without penalty.

The government influences interest rates. Along with supply and demand and banks setting their own rates, the government also plays a role in how savings account interest rates are determined. For example, when the Federal Reserve bank buys large amounts of US **Treasury securities**, it increases the demand for them, which makes them more expensive and reduces how much they pay in return. Since banks often invest in Treasurys for a safe return, lower yields—meaning banks make less money on loans and investments—can lead banks to lower the interest rates they offer on savings accounts. They may also need to lower the interest rates on loans to adjust to market conditions.

This is one way the Federal Reserve supports its goals of keeping prices stable and helping the job market stay strong. Remember, banks must compete with other savings options, so when the returns from investments like Treasurys go down, savings account rates usually drop too. However, when interest rates in the economy go up, banks may raise savings account rates to stay competitive.

Interest rates can change on savings accounts. Yes, interest rates on savings accounts can change over time. Let's say you opened a high-yield savings account when interest rates were low, and your starting rate was 1.5%. If inflation rises, and the Federal Reserve responds by increasing the federal funds rate, your bank may decide to raise your savings interest rate as well. Over the next few months, your high-yield savings account could increase to 3%, 4%, or even 5%, depending on how much rates go up. On the flip side, if the Federal Reserve lowers interest rates or starts buying large amounts of US Treasurys, your savings account rate might drop instead. This is because banks often adjust their rates based on what the Federal Reserve does and how the broader economy is performing.

You can get a higher interest rate on your savings account. Just because interest rates are going up in general doesn't mean your savings account will automatically earn more. If your current account is still paying very little interest, looking at other options may be a good idea. Start by asking your bank if they offer a different savings account with a better rate. If they don't, you may want to consider opening a high-yield savings account. These are often offered by **online-only banks**, which usually provide higher interest rates than traditional banks with physical branches. One exception is Capital One Bank, which I use for my savings. At the time of writing this book, their savings account interest rate is 4.25%, and I've even seen it reach 4.35%.

What's a CD?

A **certificate of deposit (CD)** is a type of savings account that pays a **fixed interest rate** on your money for a set period.[11] CDs are offered by both banks and credit unions. Unlike with regular savings accounts, the money you put into a CD must stay there until the end of the term you agreed on; otherwise, you'll likely have to pay a penalty. CDs usually offer higher interest rates than regular savings accounts to make up for the fact that you can't withdraw the money whenever you want. Opening a CD is like opening any other bank account, but the difference lies in the agreement you make when you open it.

After researching and choosing the right CD, the final steps—reviewing and agreeing to the terms and funding the account—will lock you into four main conditions:[12]

The interest rate. Most CDs have a fixed interest rate, though there are variable-rate CDs out there that could help you earn a higher return if rates rise. With a fixed-rate CD, you'll know exactly how much you'll earn by the end of the term, but it could hurt you if rates rise after you're locked in.

11 Jason Fernando, "What Is a Certificate of Deposit (CD) Pros and Cons," Investopedia, June 15, 2025, https://www.investopedia.com/terms/c/certificateofdeposit.asp.

12 Fernando, "What Is a Certificate of Deposit (CD) Pros and Cons."

The term. This is the amount of time you agree to keep your money in the CD without taking it out early. Common CD terms include six months, one year, eighteen months, and more. The term ends on what's called the **maturity date**. Once the CD reaches that date, it has fully matured, and you can take out your money without any penalty.

The principal. Unless you're opening a special type of CD, the principal is the amount of money you agree to deposit when the account is opened. This is often called your **initial deposit**.

The institution. When you open a CD, the bank or credit union sets rules such as **early-withdrawal penalties** and whether the CD will automatically renew when it matures. Once opened and funded, a CD works like other deposit accounts. You'll receive monthly or quarterly statements—either by mail or online—and interest is added to your balance regularly. That interest then compounds, helping your money grow over time. CDs usually offer a fixed and safe interest rate, which is often higher than what you'd get from a regular savings or money market account, especially if you're willing to leave the money in for a longer term. They're great for setting money aside for specific goals, like buying a home or a car or going on a big trip.

When choosing a CD, it's smart to consider what the Federal Reserve is doing with interest rates. If rates are expected to rise, locking into a long-term CD too early could hurt your future earnings. If rates are expected to fall, it might be a good time to lock in a higher rate. CDs are one of the safest places to keep your money for two reasons. First, the interest rate is guaranteed and does not change. Second, CDs are insured—up to $250,000—by the **Federal Deposit Insurance Corporation** (for banks) or the **National Credit Union Administration** (for credit unions). This means if your bank or credit union fails, your money is still protected. To stay safe, make sure your bank or credit union is insured by the FDIC or NCUA, and don't keep more than $250,000 in your name at any one institution.

Pros

- CDs offer a fixed interest rate, so you know exactly what you'll earn.
- They usually pay more interest than regular savings or money market accounts.
- They're safe and low risk, especially when opened at an FDIC- or NCUA-insured institution.
- CDs are good for saving for a specific goal with a set timeline.
- The interest compounds, helping your money grow faster.

Cons

- You can't withdraw your money early without paying a penalty.
- No additional deposits can be made after opening the account.
- Your money is locked in for a set period—anywhere from a few months to several years.
- If interest rates go up, your CD rate stays the same until it matures.

Do Banks Just Let My Money Sit Until I Need It, and Are There Any Fees Associated with It?

According to Bankrate, only a small amount of the money you deposit at a bank is actually held in cash.[13] Most of it is used by the bank to make **loans**—like personal or business loans, government bonds, or credit card lending. The people who borrow this money

13 Marcus Cabello, "What Banks Do with Your Money After You Deposit It," Bankrate, June 17, 2025, https://www.bankrate.com/banking/what-banks-do-with-deposits/.

have to pay it back with **interest**. That interest is how banks make a profit and generate revenue. You may remember we talked about **interest rates** earlier in this chapter.

Now, let's look at some common **fees** that can come with opening a checking or savings account. You can avoid many of these fees, especially if you become a **preferred customer** at your bank. We'll go into more detail about what that means later, but for now, here are some typical fees you should be aware of.[14]

Monthly maintenance or service fees. This is a fee some banks charge just for keeping your account open. It can often be waived if you keep a certain minimum balance or set up direct deposit.

Out-of-network ATM fees. If you use an ATM that doesn't belong to your bank, you might be charged a fee by both your bank and the ATM owner. Some banks refund this fee for preferred customers.

Overdraft fees. This fee occurs if you spend more money than you have in your account. The bank covers the difference but charges you a fee for doing so. Be very careful when writing checks, and make sure you can cover your purchases. Another phrase for this is *bouncing a check*.

Insufficient funds fees. If you write a check or make a payment and don't have enough money in your account to cover it, the bank may decline the transaction and charge you this fee.

Paper statement fees. Banks may charge you for receiving printed account statements in the mail. You can avoid this fee by logging into your online account and selecting the option to enroll in paperless statements.

Wire transfer fees. A **wire transfer** lets you send money directly to another person's bank account. Fees vary depending on whether the money is sent to the same bank, a different bank, or another country. Some banks waive or reduce fees if you send the transfer

14 Bank of America, "8 Common Bank Fees—and How to Avoid Them," Better Money Habits by Bank of America, accessed August 2025, https://bettermoneyhabits.bankofamerica.com/en/personal-banking/avoid-bank-fees.

online instead of in person. You can also avoid these fees by using apps like Zelle or Venmo. For example, I've seen barbers use Zelle to accept payments without any extra cost.

Account closing fees. Some banks charge a fee if you close your account too soon after opening it. This usually applies if the account is closed within the first 180 days, although some banks have even shorter time frames. To avoid this, try to choose a bank that fits your long-term financial needs.

Dormancy fees. A **dormant account** is one that hasn't had any activity for a long time. The bank may charge a fee if your account stays inactive. You can avoid this by making small deposits or withdrawals now and then. Another option is to set up **automatic payments** from the account to keep it active.

Foreign transaction fees. If you travel to another country and use your debit card to make purchases, you may be charged a **foreign transaction fee**. These fees are often around 1% or more of the purchase amount. Not all banks charge this fee, so it's a good idea to check with your bank before traveling. I found this out the hard way on a trip to Toronto, Canada.

Lost card fee. If you lose your bank card, your bank may charge a **replacement fee**, and possibly an extra fee to rush the delivery. When reporting a lost or stolen card, ask if the bank can waive the fee. To avoid extra charges, you can choose standard delivery and use a payment app or cash while waiting for your new card.

Will My Money Be in the Bank Even If the Bank Gets Robbed?

When you open an account at most US banks, your money is automatically protected by a type of insurance called FDIC coverage. Protection comes from the Federal Deposit Insurance Corporation, a government agency. It covers your account balance—including interest earned—up to $250,000 per person, per account type, across all your accounts at the same bank. You don't need to sign up for this coverage; it's included by default as long as your bank is FDIC-insured.[15]

15 Cabello, "What Banks Do with Your Money After You Deposit It."

What's the Difference Between a Bank and a Credit Union?

A **credit union** is a financial institution that's owned by its members, not by investors. Credit unions offer many of the same services as banks—like checking accounts, savings accounts, and loans—but often with lower fees and better interest rates.

Since they aren't focused on making a profit, credit unions often pass savings on to their members. This can mean lower rates on car loans or credit cards and higher returns on savings tools like CDs. Members of credit unions also get a voice in how the organization is run, usually through voting rights. Just as bank deposits are protected by the FDIC, credit union deposits are covered by the NCUA. Your money is insured—up to $250,000 per person, per account, if the credit union is insured by the NCUA.[16] This insurance is automatic and keeps your funds safe, even if the credit union fails.

What's an Online Bank Account?

Online banking lets you manage your money using the internet, anytime—day or night.[17] You can use it to do most things you would normally do at a regular bank branch. This includes making deposits, transferring money, and paying bills online. You can access your account using a computer, tablet, or smartphone.

What's a Direct Deposit; Will It Benefit Me to Have One?

Direct deposit is when money is sent electronically to your bank account instead of via a paper check.[18] This process uses a system called the **Automated Clearing House**, which moves money safely between banks. Many employers use direct deposit to pay their workers. To set it up, you'll need to give the payer your bank's name, your account number, and the routing number for your bank. We

---

16 Lita Epstein, "Credit Unions vs. Banks: What's the Difference?," Investopedia, November 9, 2024, https://www.investopedia.com/credit-unions-vs-banks-4590218.

17 Lorraine Roberte, "What Is Online Banking? Definition and How It Works," Investopedia, February 28, 2025, https://www.investopedia.com/terms/o/onlinebanking.asp.

18 Julia Kagan, "Direct Deposit: What It Is, How It Works, Benefits & Risks?," Investopedia, March 12, 2024, https://www.investopedia.com/terms/d/directdeposit.asp.

spoke about account numbers and routing numbers earlier. They can easily be found on your checks for your checking account. Direct deposits are a huge advantage for receiving your monthly wages from work or having your income tax return automatically deposited into your bank account.

What's a Bank's Preferred Customer, and What Are the Benefits of Being One?

According to Bank of America, becoming a **preferred customer** at your bank can come with many benefits, but it's not a title that's given to just anyone. To qualify, you usually need to keep a **minimum balance** across your accounts. In some cases, this means having as much as $20,000 or more in combined daily balances over several months. Once you reach that status, you may get access to special perks on loans, savings accounts, and other financial services.

Talk to your bank to find out exactly what it takes to qualify. Some of the common benefits include these perks:[19]

- Lower or no monthly fees. Preferred customers often don't pay the standard maintenance fees on checking or savings accounts.
- Higher interest rates on savings. You may earn better returns on savings accounts, CDs, or money market accounts.
- Reduced loan rates. Some banks offer lower interest rates on personal loans, mortgages, or auto loans for preferred customers.
- ATM fee refunds. You may be reimbursed for out-of-network ATM fees, including fees charged by other banks.

19 Bank of America, "Bank of America Preferred Rewards," accessed July 7, 2025, https://promotions.bankofamerica.com/preferredrewards/en#requirements.

- Priority customer service. Preferred customers often get access to dedicated service lines or even a personal banker.
- Discounted or waived wire transfer fees. Domestic or international wire transfers may come with reduced or no fees.

CHAPTER 1 TAKEAWAYS

You should now have a better understanding of the following:

- ✓ **Checking and savings account differences.** Understanding the fundamental differences between checking and savings accounts, including their unique purposes and how they support personal money management, will help you use each account effectively.
- ✓ **Benefits of maintaining both accounts.** Recognizing the practical benefits of maintaining both types of accounts, such as easier budgeting, access to emergency funds, and safer money handling, can strengthen your overall financial organization.
- ✓ **Basic banking operations.** Becoming familiar with basic banking operations, including how to write checks, make deposits, and withdraw funds securely, will help you manage everyday transactions with confidence.
- ✓ **How banks generate revenue.** Gaining insight into how banks make money, the importance of interest rates, and how your money is protected through federal deposit insurance will deepen your understanding of the banking system.
- ✓ **Common account types and services**. Identifying different account types and common banking services, such as direct deposits, ATM access, and preferred customer benefits, will help you take full advantage of available banking features.

Source: Your Blueprint for Financial Literacy

Chapter 2

What Are Utility Bills?

Utilities are essential services that are offered to the general public. These can include electricity, gas, water, sewer, and trash pickup.[20] In my view, internet and cable also count as utilities in today's world.

Even though these services are available to the public, they aren't free—you have to pay for what you use. Utility bills are usually due monthly and are separate from your rent or mortgage, unless included in a rental agreement, which isn't common. The utility company charges you based on how much of the service you use. Your bill might come as a paper copy by mail or as a digital version by email or through the provider's website; that choice is up to you. Most utility bills include your name, address, account number, amount due, and the due date. They also explain how you can pay—by check, online, phone, or through **direct debit**. Direct debit means the money is automatically taken from your bank account to cover the bill.

Q&A SESSION

What's a Water Bill; I Thought Water Was Free?

A water bill is usually sent each month by the company that supplies water to your home. In some areas, it may also be called a sewer

20 PropertyClub Team, "What Is a Utility Bill: Guide and Costs," PropertyClub (blog), June 12, 2022, https://propertyclub.nyc/article/what-is-a-utility-bill-guide-and-costs.

bill, depending on how the services are combined. This bill shows how much water you've used over the last billing period and what you owe for that usage. Anything in your home that uses water—like showers, baths, sinks, toilets, dishwashers, or even an outdoor hose—adds to your total. Water usage is measured in gallons, and your total bill is based on how many gallons you used multiplied by your provider's rate per gallon. To keep your bill lower, try not to let water run unnecessarily or drip from faucets, as this can waste water and raise your costs.

What's an Electric Bill?

An electric bill—also called a power bill or electricity bill—is a monthly statement you receive from your electric company that shows how much electricity you've used—measured in kilowatt-hours—and how much you owe.[21] Any power used by devices in your home adds to this total. This includes things like charging your phone, watching TV, using lights, running the air conditioner, or cooking on an electric stove. To help lower your bill, turn off lights when you're not using them and unplug cords from outlets you're not actively using. In some countries, like the United Kingdom, wall outlets have switches that stop electricity from flowing even when something is plugged in. You simply flip the switch to the off position. Since this feature isn't common in the US, it's still a good habit to unplug unused electronics.

What's a Gas Bill?

First, it's important to understand what natural gas is. This isn't like the gas you put in your car. According to the US Energy Information Administration, natural gas is a type of fossil fuel, mostly made up of methane. It doesn't have an odor or color, so gas companies add a chemical called mercaptan that gives it a strong rotten-egg smell. This helps people detect gas leaks in or around their homes.

21 Shop Solar, "Electric Bill: Definition & Meaning," accessed July 7, 2025, https://shopsolarkits.com/pages/electric-bill-definition.

Natural gas travels through a system of pipelines across the country and is regulated and measured before it reaches your home.[22] Some appliances that could run off natural gas include your oven and stove, laundry machines, furnace, air conditioner, water heaters, and fireplaces. Many homes use a mix of electricity and gas. For example, you may have a gas oven but an electric washer and dryer.

Be mindful if you have gas appliances. Always turn off your oven after use, and if you ever smell that rotten-egg odor, call 911 or your local emergency services right away.

What's Green Energy, and Do I Have to Pay for It?

According to the National Grid, the terms *green energy* and *renewable energy* are often used the same way, but there is an important difference between them. Most green energy sources are renewable, but not all renewable energy is completely green. **Renewable energy** comes from natural sources that are always being replenished, like sunlight, wind, and water. You might also hear it called **sustainable energy** because it doesn't run out the way fossil fuels do.[23] However, not every renewable source is considered "green" if it still has some impact on the environment—like producing carbon emissions when building the equipment needed to generate the power.

According to Energy.gov, the way we get electricity in the US is changing.[24] At the time of writing this book, over half of all electricity customers could choose to get power from renewable sources through their energy provider. Even if your provider doesn't offer that option directly, everyone can support clean energy by purchasing **renewable energy certificates**. You may have heard this kind of electricity called **green power** or **clean power**. If you

22 U.S. Energy Information Administration, "Natural Gas Explained," Energy Explained, last updated October 10, 2024, https://www.eia.gov/energyexplained/natural-gas/.

23 National Grid, "What Is Green Energy?," last updated August 9, 2023, https://www.nationalgrid.com/stories/energy-explained/what-is-green-energy.

24 U.S. Department of Energy, "Buying Renewable Electricity," Consumer Savings, accessed December 19, 2025, https://www.energy.gov/energysaver/buying-renewable-electricity.

drive an electric vehicle, you're likely using green energy to charge your battery—especially if it comes from solar or wind power. If you've seen solar panels on rooftops or buildings, that's another example of green energy in action. Depending on where you live, you might be able to support clean power through one or more of the following programs:[25]

Green pricing. Some utility companies offer a service where you pay a small extra fee to receive electricity from renewable sources. This helps the cost for the company to add more clean energy—like wind or solar—to their power supply.

Competitive electricity markets. In certain states, the electricity market is open to competition. This means you can choose who supplies your power and how it's generated. Some clean energy companies specialize in selling renewable electricity to homes and businesses. Even traditional suppliers may partner with them to give you more green power options.

Green certificates. If your local provider doesn't offer clean power, you can still support it by buying green certificates. Also called renewable energy certificates or green tags, these allow you to contribute to clean energy projects—no matter where you live. Each certificate represents a certain amount of electricity made from renewable sources and helps increase the amount of clean energy in the overall grid.

What's a Broadband Service Provider?

If you didn't know already, internet use can contribute to the cost of your electric bill. However, this service doesn't come from your electricity service provider but from your internet or broadband service provider. Like electricity or gas, though, you're charged for the services you subscribe to. Broadband services include cable TV, internet, and telephone. Some well-known broadband service providers are Verizon, Optimum, and Dish (in partnership with AT&T).

25 National Grid, "What Is Green Energy?"

According to the Federal Communications Commission, broadband or high-speed internet access allows users to access the internet and internet-related services at significantly higher speeds than those available through dial-up services. Broadband speeds vary significantly depending on the technology and level of service ordered. Broadband services for residential consumers typically provide faster downstream speeds (from the internet to your computer) than upstream speeds (from your computer to the internet). The faster the speed, the more the cost to the customer. If you bundle your service together, meaning you get all broadband services from the same provider, it will usually cost less overall.[26]

Can I Be Forced to Pay Utility Bills; What Happens If I Refuse to Pay My Utility Bills?

Not paying your utility bill could lead to your electricity, gas, or water being shut off. Before doing so, they are required to give you a written notice letting you know they plan to disconnect your service. They must also wait at least fifteen days after the notice to give you a chance to pay the overdue amount or set up a payment plan. Keep these important things in mind:

Final termination notice. If you haven't paid your utility bill, a deposit, or a payment agreement, the utility company must send you a **final termination notice** before shutting off your service. This notice will explain why your service might be turned off, list the earliest date it could happen, and include the utility's contact information. It will also mention your rights under the Home Energy Fair Practices Act. The utility can send this notice twenty days after the missed payment due date. Once the notice is sent, they must give you fifteen more days to fix the issue before they can disconnect your service. But if you pay by check and the check is returned or rejected by the bank, the utility can shut off your service without sending another notice.

26 Federal Communications Commission, "Getting Broadband Q&A," Consumer Guides, January 25, 2024, https://www.fcc.gov/consumers/guides/getting-broadband-qa.

When service can be shut off. Utilities can shut off your service only between the hours of 8 a.m. and 4 p.m. from Monday through Thursday. However, even if you haven't paid your bill, there are certain situations where the utility company is not allowed to disconnect your service:[27]

1. You haven't received a final termination notice from the utility.
2. The amount owed is over a year old, and the delay in action was not your fault.
3. A doctor certifies to the utility that someone in the home has a medical emergency.
4. You have a billing dispute with the utility or the Public Service Commission, and you've already paid the portion of the bill that isn't being disputed.
5. You pay the full amount owed at the time the utility comes to shut off service.
6. You set up a payment agreement with the utility to cover what you owe.
7. Service also cannot be shut off on a public holiday, the day before a holiday, during the two-week period including Christmas and New Year's Day, or on a day before the utility office is closed.

What's the Best Way to Pay My Utility Bills?

You have several options when it comes to paying your utility bills. Choose the one that works best for your lifestyle and helps you avoid missed payments:

27 New York State Department of Public Service, "Your Rights as a Residential Gas, Electric or Steam Customer Under HEFPA," Consumer Publications, accessed July 2, 2025, https://dps.ny.gov/consumer-guide-your-rights-residential-gas-electric-or-steam-customer-under-hefpa.

- Online. Most service providers let you create an online account. You can set up direct debit to have your bill paid automatically from your checking account. This is how I pay all my utility bills—it's quick, easy, and helps avoid late payments or service shutoffs.
- By phone. Call the customer service number listed on your bill. You'll usually be guided through a secure system to make a payment using your credit card or bank information.
- In person. You can go to your utility company's local office and pay using cash, check, money order, debit, or credit card.
- By mail. You can also send a check or money order by mail to the address listed on your bill. Make sure to mail it early so it arrives before the due date.

CHAPTER 2 TAKEAWAYS

You should now have a better understanding of the following:

- ✓ **Comprehensive overview of utilities.** Understanding the different types of utility bills—like water, electricity, gas, and internet—and what they cost can help you keep track of your usage, spot where you might be wasting money, and possibly bring those bills down.
- ✓ **Cost awareness.** Addressing misconceptions about free utilities will help you budget more effectively for essential services.
- ✓ **Consequences of nonpayment.** Understanding what happens if you refuse to pay utility bills will prepare you to avoid potential issues with service providers.
- ✓ **Payment strategies.** Tips on the best ways to pay utility bills will empower you to manage your expenses efficiently.

Source: Your Blueprint for Financial Literacy

Chapter 3

Should I Get a Credit Card, and How Are Interest Rates Related to Credit Cards?

First, it's important to know what a credit card is. A credit card is a plastic or metal card that lets you borrow money from a bank or financial company to make purchases. You can use it to pay for things anywhere credit cards are accepted. Whatever you spend, you'll have to pay back—either in full by the due date or over time. But if you don't pay it all off, you'll likely be charged interest and maybe even late fees.

Understanding credit cards and how they work is essential. Credit cards can be a lifesaver, but, at the same time, your worst nightmare if you lack the proper knowledge of their rules. They can create a moment of pleasure, which in turn can result in a lifetime of pain if they are misused. There are several types of credit card providers out there. Usually, they are issued by retail banks. Some well-known credit cards are Mastercard, Visa, American Express, and Discover. Pay close attention to this section to get a good understanding of credit cards and how they work.

Q&A SESSION

How Do I Get a Credit Card?

According to Capital One Bank, before applying for a credit card, it's important to know *why* you want one. There are many types of cards available, and the right one for you depends on your **financial goals**. Ask yourself these questions:[28]

- What are your financial goals? Credit cards can help with things like building credit or earning rewards. If you're looking at a card with an annual fee, think about whether the benefits or rewards are worth the cost. Learn about the card's APR and how to avoid paying interest.
- Do you want to build or rebuild credit? Any credit card can help improve your credit if used the right way. If you're just starting out, a secured card—which requires a cash deposit as collateral—may be easier to get. That deposit usually becomes your credit limit, making it less risky for the lender.
- Are you trying to pay off debt? Some cards offer low or 0% APR for a limited time on balance transfers. This can help you move high-interest debt to a new card and save money. Just watch for transfer fees and know when the introductory rate ends.
- Do you have a big purchase coming up? You might use a card with 0% APR to spread out payments over time. This can help if you plan carefully, but be sure you can pay it off before interest kicks in.
- Do you plan to travel internationally? If so, look for a card with no foreign transaction fees—that way you're not charged extra every time you make a purchase overseas.

Keep these key things in mind when applying for a credit card: If you're young or new to the United States, it's important to know that credit cards are a common part of life here. Even if you don't

28 Andrew Bloomenthal, "Credit Card: What It Is, How It Works, and How to Get One," Investopedia, September 30, 2024, https://www.investopedia.com/terms/c/creditcard.asp.

have one yet, getting a card can be a first step in building credit. That's why making on-time payments is crucial—it helps build a strong credit history. According to Capital One Bank, you can take six steps to help you get a credit card:[29]

Step 1. Check your credit report. You can check your **credit score** through credit bureaus like Experian and Equifax. A **credit report** is a summary of your credit activity—like loans, credit card accounts, and payment history.[30] Most people have more than one report, and not all lenders report to every bureau. Lenders use your credit report and score to decide whether they'll approve you for a loan or credit card and what interest rate you'll get. Other companies may check your report (with your permission) when you apply for housing, insurance, utilities, or even a job. Knowing your score helps you understand which cards you're more likely to be approved for—even if your score isn't perfect. Checking your credit regularly can help you catch mistakes or fraud early. Your credit report includes these items:

- Personal information, like your name (and past names), address, birth date, Social Security number, and phone number
- Credit account information, such as credit type (like loans or cards), limits, balances, payment history, open and close dates, and the lender's name
- Collections data, like missed payments, unpaid loans, or overdue child support sent to collections
- Public records, including bankruptcies, liens, foreclosures, and court judgments
- Inquiries, such as companies that have checked your credit report

29 Capital One, "How to Get a Credit Card," February 6, 2025, https://www.capitalone.com/learn-grow/money-management/how-to-apply-for-a-credit-card/.

30 Consumer Financial Protection Bureau, "What Is a Credit Report?," Credit Reports and Scores, January 29, 2024, https://www.consumerfinance. gov/ask-cfpb/what-is-a-credit-report-en-309/.

Step 2. Explore credit cards. Before choosing a card, take time to learn how credit cards work and compare things like interest rates, fees, and rewards. Using a card responsibly—like paying your bill on time each month—can help you build credit over time. There are many types of credit cards to choose from, depending on your goals:

- Cash back cards allow you to earn a percentage of money back on everyday purchases.
- Travel rewards cards help you earn miles or points for travel expenses.
- Secured cards are great for building or rebuilding credit; they require a refundable deposit.
- Student cards are designed for college students to start building credit while earning rewards.
- Low introductory-rate cards are helpful for paying off debt or avoiding interest for a limited time.
- Business cards are made for small businesses to manage expenses and earn rewards.

Step 3. Understand the requirements needed to apply. When you apply for a credit card, you may be asked to provide documents to prove your identity, age, and residency. Requirements can vary from one credit card company to another, but they'll consider common factors like these:

Age. You must be at least eighteen years old to apply for a credit card in your own name. If you're under twenty-one, you'll need to show proof that you have enough income to make your payments on your own—or apply with a **cosigner** who is twenty-one or older. Keep in mind, not all credit card companies accept cosigners. We'll talk more about cosigners in chapter 5.

Personal information. You might be asked to show documents like a driver's license, passport, green card, or birth certificate. Some credit card companies also require proof of your income and US residence to process your application.

Step 4. Find out whether you're preapproved. Preapproval is a helpful way to see which credit cards you might qualify for *without hurting your credit score*. It allows you to compare different options and find a card that's a good match before you officially apply. When a credit card offer says you're **prequalified** or **preapproved**, it usually means that your credit score and some of your financial details meet the basic requirements for that card. For example, with Capital One, the preapproval process is fast, only asks for basic information, and does not affect your credit score.

Step 5. Submit your credit card application. There are a few ways to apply for a credit card. Choose the one that works best for you:

- Online. This is often the fastest method. You may get an instant decision, and if approved, some banks may even give you a virtual card number to use right away.
- In person. You can apply at a bank branch or a Capital One Café, where a staff member can help you with the application and answer questions.
- By phone. Calling to apply can be almost as quick as applying online, but you might have to wait on hold, depending on the time of day.
- By mail. This is usually the slowest option. You'll have to wait for your application to be delivered and then wait again for the decision to be mailed back to you.

Step 6. Use your card responsibly. Getting approved for a credit card is a great first step. If used wisely, it can help you build strong credit and manage your spending. Follow these tips to use your card responsibly:

- Always pay on time to avoid late fees, interest rate increases, and damage to your credit.
- Consider setting up automatic payments or reminders so you don't forget.
- If possible, pay your full balance each month. This helps your credit score and saves on interest.
- If you can't pay the full amount, pay as much as you can but at least the minimum due.

Many banks, including Capital One, offer tools to help you get started with your first card. To track your credit score, apps like Credit Karma can be helpful. You can download it on your phone or use it on your computer to keep an eye on your progress.

How Does a Credit Card Work?

As summarized by Lyle Daly of The Motley Fool, a credit card gives you access to funds from a bank or lender that you can use to pay for things, instead of using your own cash up front. Any place that accepts credit cards will let you make purchases with the card. Some cards also allow cash withdrawals, but those usually come with extra fees, so it's best to avoid them unless necessary. When you use a credit card, the amount you spend is recorded by the lender.[31]

For example, if you swipe your card to buy something for $250, that amount gets added to what you owe the lender. Every card has a spending cap—this is the highest total you're allowed to borrow at one time. Let's say your card has a limit of $2,000. If you've spent $250, you still have $1,750 left that you can use. As

31 Matt Koppenheffer, "Best Credit Cards of August 2025," Motley Fool Money, accessed August 1, 2025, https://www.fool.com/the-ascent/credit-cards/articles/how-do-credit-cards-work/.

you pay down what you owe, the money becomes available again for future use. That means you can continue using the same card, as long as you're making payments and still have room under your spending cap. Table 3.1 highlights the differences between a debit card and a credit card:

Table 3.1 Comparison of Debit and Credit Cards

Feature	Debit Card	Credit Card
Source of funds	Money comes directly from your bank account	Money is borrowed from the card issuer
Spending limit	Limited to your account balance	Limited to your credit limit
Monthly payments	None	Yes
Interest charges	None	Interest applies if balance isn't paid in full
Effect on credit history	Does not build credit	Can help build credit with responsible use
Overdraft risk	Possible if you opt into overdraft protection	No overdraft but spending beyond limit is declined
Rewards or perks	Rarely offers rewards	Often offers rewards, points, or cash back
Effect on credit score	None	Affects credit score based on usage and payments
Best for	Everyday purchases using your own money	Building credit and earning rewards

Table 3.1 Source: Your Blueprint for Financial Literacy

Can I Buy Anything with a Credit Card?

These days, you can use a credit card for almost any type of purchase, with several benefits to doing so. One major advantage is that most credit cards offer fraud protection. If someone uses your card without permission, you're usually not responsible for the charges—this makes it safer than carrying cash or even using a debit card.

Another benefit is that many credit cards offer rewards for your spending. This could include cash back, points, or travel miles, which can help offset your costs. But credit cards also come with risks, especially if you carry a balance month to month.[32] At the time this book was written, Forbes Advisor reported that the average credit card interest rate on accounts carrying a balance was approximately 25.34% as of May 2025—and that can add up fast.[33] So it's important to use your card wisely and to avoid using it in ways that could lead to long-term debt.

Your spending habits and your ability to pay off purchases will help you decide when it's better to use credit, debit, or cash. When used responsibly, credit cards can help you earn rewards on everyday expenses like these:

- Clothing
- Gas
- Groceries
- Kids' sports equipment
- School fees
- Toiletries
- Utility bills

32 Holly Johnson, "Which Purchases Should Go on Your Credit Card?," CNET Money, August 4, 2023, https://www.cnet.com/personal-finance/credit-cards/which-purchases-should-go-on-your-credit-card/.

33 Evan Coleman, "What Is The Average Credit Card Interest Rate This Week?," Forbes Advisor, August 4, 2025, https://www.forbes.com/advisor/credit-cards/average-credit-card-interest-rate/.

For some bills—like utilities—you may be charged an extra fee for paying with a credit card instead of a bank transfer or debit. In those cases, it's smart to compare the fee to the value of the rewards you'd earn. Also, don't overspend just to earn rewards. If you can't pay off the full amount, you'll be charged interest, which could cancel out the value of any rewards you earned. And don't forget about annual fees or other costs some cards charge. That word *interest* keeps showing up because it *really* matters!

What's the Difference Between a Credit Card and a Store Card?

Have you ever been at the register at Macy's or JCPenney and heard *Would you like to apply for a store card and get an extra 15% off today's purchase?* If so, you're not alone; almost everyone gets asked that at some point. Here's the deal: A **store card** is like a credit card, but it usually only works at that store. Retailers partner with banks to offer these cards to encourage you to spend more now and pay later. That sounds nice in the moment, but you really need to know a few things about store cards:[34]

There are two kinds of store cards. The kind of card you have determines where you can use it. **Closed-loop cards** only work at that store, like Macy's or Raymour & Flanigan. **Open-loop cards** have a Visa, Mastercard, or American Express logo, so you can use them almost anywhere.[35]

Store cards still charge interest. Store cards often have high interest rates. If you don't pay the full balance, you'll get charged interest just like with credit cards—sometimes even more. Look for offers that say *no interest for X months*, and try to pay off the full amount before that time is up.

It may be easier to get a store card. Store cards are often easier to qualify for, even with low or limited credit. That's why cashiers

34 Lee Huffman, "What's the Difference Between a Store Card and a Credit Card?," Forbes Advisor, February 26, 2025, https://www.forbes.com/advisor/credit-cards/whats-the-difference-between-a-store-card-and-a-credit-card/.

35 Troy Segal, "Open Loop Card: What It Is, How It Works?," Investopedia, February 25, 2024, https://www.investopedia.com/terms/o/open-loop-card.asp.

push them hard. You might even get **instant approval** at the register with just your ID and Social Security number. Store cards can be a good starter option for building credit—but only if used wisely.

Store cards work like a credit card, with one exception. You get a **spending limit** and can make charges up to that amount. As you pay it down, you free up credit again—just like with a credit card. The difference? You're usually locked into one brand or store.

Store cards can hurt your credit. If you miss payments or max out the card, your credit score could take a hit. To help build credit, pay on time and keep your balance low. Treat a store card as you would a regular credit card: with care and attention.

> A store card can be a helpful tool if used responsibly. But if mismanaged, it can hurt more than help.

What's an Interest Rate?

You've seen the term *interest rate* mentioned several times already, so let's take a moment to really understand what it means. In simple terms, an **interest rate** is the price you pay to borrow money.[36] For example, when you take out a loan for a car or home, the lender charges you interest on the amount you borrow. On the flip side, when you deposit money into a savings account or a certificate of deposit, the bank pays you interest for keeping your money there—because they use those funds to lend to others. Banks like Capital One are known to offer competitive interest rates on savings, making them appealing for everyday savers. Interest rates are generally shown as a **percentage per year**, also known as the **annual rate**. And according to Investopedia, interest is the charge made for using someone else's asset.

That asset could be money, but it might also be goods, vehicles, or real estate. That's why interest is often referred to as the **cost**

36 Caroline Banton, "Interest Rates: Types and What They Mean to Borrowers," Investopedia, May 11, 2025, https://www.investopedia.com/terms/i/interestrate.asp.

of using money—the higher the interest rate, the more it costs to borrow the same amount. There are different types of interest rates, and knowing the difference can help you make better financial decisions.[37] Let's take a look:

Simple interest rate. Let's say you take out a $180,000 loan from the bank, and the agreement says you'll pay 5% interest per year using simple interest. Here's how that would look after one year:

Simple interest equals the principal multiplied by interest rate and time.

$$\$180{,}000 \times 5\% \times 1 \text{ year} = \$9{,}000$$

That means after one year, you'll owe the bank $189,000 ($180,000 plus $9,000).

Now let's look at a longer loan—say it's for twenty years at that same 5% interest rate. Here's the formula for total interest you'd pay over that time:

$$\$180{,}000 \times 5\% \times 20 \text{ years} = \$180{,}000$$

So in total, you'd repay $360,000 ($180,000 loan plus $180,000 interest).

This is how simple interest works—and it's a clear example of how banks earn money over time through loans and mortgages. You're not just paying back what you borrowed; you're also paying for the cost of borrowing.

Compound interest rate. Some lenders use **compound interest**, which means you'll pay more over time compared to simple interest. Here's how it works: Instead of calculating interest only on the original loan amount, compound interest is charged on both the principal and the interest that builds up over time.[38] So,

37 Banton, "Interest Rates: Types and What They Mean to Borrowers."

38 Jason Fernando, "The Power of Compound Interest: Calculations and Examples," Investopedia, updated June 14, 2025, https://www.investopedia.com/terms/c/compoundinterest.asp.

after the first year, you owe the loan amount plus interest. By the second year, interest is calculated not only on your loan but also on the interest from the previous year. This cycle continues—year after year—which is why people call it **interest on interest**. Yes, it adds up quickly! That's an eye-opener, isn't it?

Now, let's go back to our example: You borrowed $180,000 at 5% interest over twenty years. With simple interest, you'd pay about $180,000 in interest, bringing your total repayment to around $360,000. But with compounding, the interest builds over time—you'd end up paying closer to $297,593.59 in interest, for a total repayment of about $477,593.59. That's significantly more than the original loan.

Use the following formula to calculate compound interest:

Total interest = loan amount × [(1 + rate of interest) to the power of time periods − 1]

- Loan amount: $180,000
- Interest rate: 5% annually
- Loan term: 20 years
- Compounding rate: annually

Total interest owed: $297,593.59
Total repayment (loan plus interest): $477,593.59

Step-by-Step Breakdown of Compound Interest Calculation
We're calculating the total repayment for a loan of $180,000 at a 5% annual interest rate over 20 years, compounded annually.

Formula
Total repayment = loan amount × (1 + interest rate)^years

Step-by-Step

1. Add 1 to the annual interest rate:
   $1 + 0.05 = 1.05$
2. Raise the result to the power of 20 (the number of years):
   $1.05^{\wedge}20 \approx 2.6533$
3. Multiply the result by the loan amount:
   $180{,}000 \times 2.6533 \approx 477{,}593.59$

Final Answer

Total repayment ≈ $477,593.59
Total interest paid = $477,593.59 - $180,000 = $297,593.59

Compound interest and savings accounts. When it comes to saving money, compound interest works in your favor. That's because the bank pays you interest on both your original deposit and any interest you've already earned—so your money keeps growing. Let's say you put $50,000 into a high-yield savings account. The bank might take $30,000 of that and loan it out as part of a home mortgage.

To make it worth your while, the bank pays you 4% interest on your savings. Meanwhile, they're charging the borrower 7% interest on that loan. That means the bank is making a 3% profit on the money it borrowed from you and lent to someone else. In simple terms, you're lending money to the bank, and they pay you for the opportunity to use it. The longer you leave your money in the account, the more it grows thanks to compound interest. If you deposit $50,000 into a high-yield savings account that pays 4% interest annually, and you leave it alone for fifteen years, your account could grow to about $90,047. That means you would earn $40,047 in interest—*without adding another penny.*

That's the power of compound interest: Your money makes money, and that money makes more money. Again, as Aunt Little Bit would say, "Now, ain't that something for your money!" Refer to figure 3.1 for an illustration of compound interest.

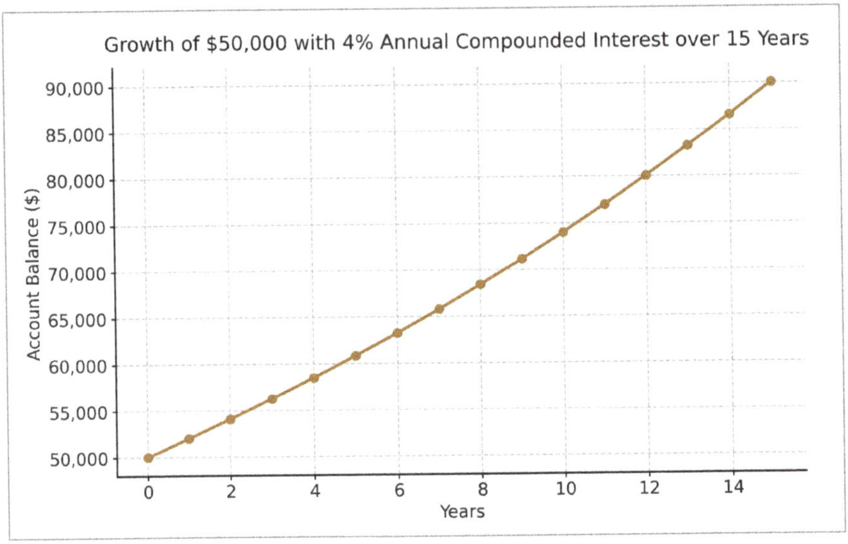

Figure 3.1 Source: Your Blueprint for Financial Literacy

Understanding APR versus APY. Yes, I know we discussed APR and APY before, but we are going into more specifics here. When you borrow money, whether through a loan or a credit card, you'll usually see the interest expressed as an APR. This is the rate the lender charges you over a year for using their money. So, if a mortgage loan has a 4% APR, that's the amount of interest charged before any compounding is factored in. APR doesn't include compounding—it just reflects the flat rate over twelve months. On the flip side, when you earn interest from your savings account or a CD, you'll see something called APY. APY includes compounding, which means it reflects the total return you'll earn over a year, including interest earned on the interest.[39] This is why APY is often a bit higher than the APR, even if the percentage rate looks the same. Refer to Figure 3.2 for an illustration comparison of APR and APY.

39 Banton, "Interest Rates: Types and What They Mean to Borrowers."

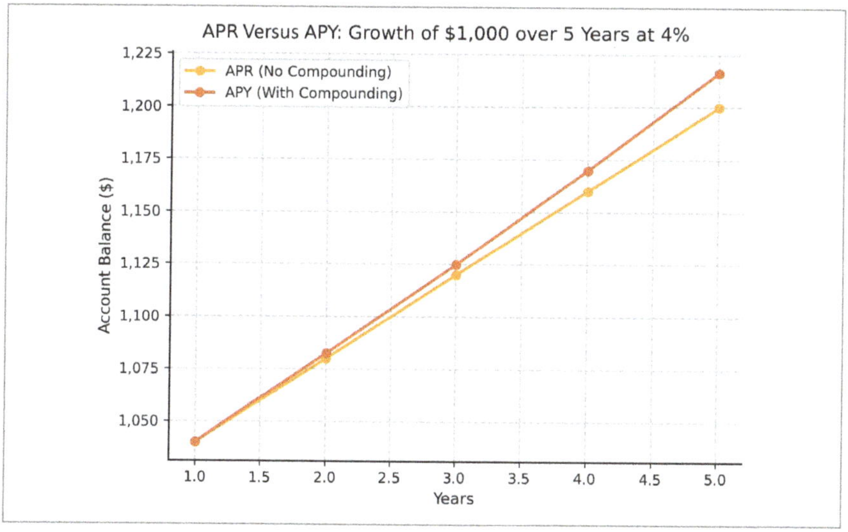

Figure 3.2 Source: Your Blueprint for Financial Literacy

What's the Difference Between Fixed and Variable Interest Rates?

If you're considering any kind of loan, whether a mortgage, car loan, or credit card, knowing the difference between fixed and variable interest rates is important. This understanding can help you avoid costly mistakes and better manage your financial goals.

A **variable interest rate** changes over time based on a market index. When interest rates drop, your loan payment may go down. But when they rise, your payment goes up. I avoid these because they can lead to unexpected payment increases. A **fixed interest rate** stays the same throughout the life of the loan. You always know what your monthly payment will be, which makes budgeting easier.[40]

No matter which type you choose, try to pay more toward the principal when you can, especially on big loans like a mortgage or auto loan. This helps you pay the balance off faster and reduces

40 Matt Lee, "Fixed and Variable Rate Loans: Which Is Better?," Investopedia, July 19, 2024, https://www.investopedia.com/ask/answers/07/fixed-variable.asp.

the total interest you'll pay. Watch out for early-payoff penalties. My mother had to hire a lawyer after being penalized for paying off her mortgage early. Always ask questions and read the contract thoroughly before signing.

Pros and Cons of Variable-Rate Loans[41]

Pros

- Potential for lower payments if interest rates fall
- Lower initial rates and better short-term perks
- Initial payments often cheaper than fixed-rate loans

Cons

- Potential for higher payments if interest rates go up
- Budgeting difficulties due to rate changes
- Potential trouble if your home value drops below the loan balance

Pros and Cons of Fixed-Rate Loans

Pros

- Steady monthly payments
- Protection from rate increases
- Ability to choose your loan term up front

Cons

- No benefit when interest rates drop

41 Lee, "Fixed and Variable Rate Loans: Which Is Better?"

- Additional expenses or difficulties to change terms
- Higher long-term costs compared to variable-rate loans

How Do I Get the Best Interest Rates on My Purchases?

If you want a lower interest rate on your credit card, one approach is to ask for one. Depending on your situation, the answer you receive may vary. If you improve your credit score, that could also be helpful. Shopping around for other cards is another way, but be sure you understand the terms and conditions and that those terms and conditions work out in your favor.

What's a FICO or Credit Score, and How Does It Affect Me?

According to the Consumer Financial Protection Bureau, a **FICO score**—also known as a credit score—is a number used to estimate how likely you are to repay borrowed money. It's a way for banks and financial institutions to figure out how likely you are to pay them back. Whether you're applying for a credit card, a car loan, or a mortgage, this score plays a big role in their decision. The term *FICO* comes from Fair Isaac Corporation, the company that created the scoring model. Some banks even use your score when deciding whether to approve you for bank accounts—not just loans.[42]

Your score is calculated based on the information in your credit report, which keeps track of how you've handled credit in the past. There are three main companies that gather this information: Experian, Equifax, and TransUnion. Each one might have slightly different data, which is why your score can look a little different depending on who pulls it. Your credit score isn't random; it's built from five main areas that show how you've handled money in the past. Understanding these factors can help you take control of your credit and improve it over time. Figure 3.3 shows what goes into your credit score.

42 Consumer Financial Protection Bureau, "What Is a FICO Score?," September 3, 2020, https://www.consumerfinance.gov/ask-cfpb/what-is-a-fico-score-en-1883/.

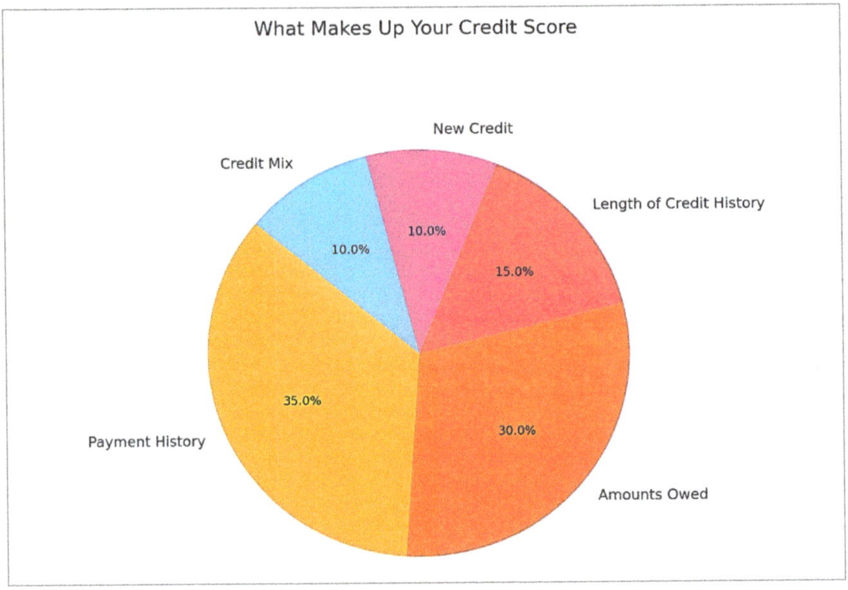

Figure 3.3 Source: Your Blueprint for Financial Literacy

What's a Late Fee?

If you have a credit card, avoid late fees at all costs. Most companies will charge you a late fee if they don't receive at least the minimum payment by the due date. And no, postmark dates don't count—the payment must be received, not just mailed, by the deadline. Here's why late fees can really hurt you:[43]

- If your payment is significantly late, your card issuer might raise your interest rate to what's called a **penalty APR**, which can apply to both current and future balances.
- The late fee itself gets added to your balance—so now you're also paying interest on that fee.

43 Deb Hipp, "What Is a Late Fee?," Credit Karma, updated November 7, 2025, https://www.creditkarma.com/advice/i/what-is-a-late-fee.

- If the payment is late enough, it could show up on your credit report, which can lower your credit score.

Moral of the story? Pay on time. Always. Even better, set up autopay or reminders to help you stay on track.

Should I Pay the Minimum Amount Due on My Credit Card Every Month?

We've talked about the importance of paying your credit card on time. My advice would be like almost any financial advice entity's: Making the minimum payment on your credit card will keep the account current and in good standing. Again, consider paying off as much of your balance as you can each month. The lower your balances, the better your credit health.

When it comes to paying off your credit card balances, you have multiple options. Paying the minimum on a credit card can be tempting. Why pay more if you don't have to? If times are tough and you've been relying on your credit cards to help you pay other bills, it's understandable if you feel you can only afford the minimum payment temporarily. Paying the balance in full, however, is best when you're able. It may help prevent your credit score from lowering and can save you money in the long term.[44]

44 TransUnion, "Paying the Balance vs. Paying the Minimum on a Credit Card," Debt Management, TransUnion Blog, updated January 15, 2024, https://www.transunion.com/blog/debt-management/credit-card-101-paying-the-balance-vs-paying-the-minimum.

CHAPTER 3 TAKEAWAYS

You should now have a better understanding of the following:

- ✓ **Informed decision-making.** Knowing how to responsibly obtain and use credit cards and weigh the benefits and drawbacks of credit enables you to build good credit.
- ✓ **Financial literacy.** Understanding interest rates, late fees, and credit scores will empower you to navigate credit effectively and maintain a good credit profile.
- ✓ **Ways to maximize benefits.** Insights into different types of credit cards will help you choose the best card for your spending habits and financial goals.
- ✓ **Payment strategies.** Knowledge about minimum payments will guide you in managing your credit card debts wisely.

Source: Your Blueprint for Financial Literacy

Chapter 4

What Is Insurance, and Do I Need It?

Comedian Chris Rock once described insurance as "just in case."[45] It's something you buy just in case something happens. Depending on the situation, insurance can literally be a lifesaver. There are so many different types out there, and no one kind covers all issues or incidents. At some point in life, almost everyone will need some form of insurance—whether it's for health, a car, a home, or their loved ones. Insurance can be either expensive or cheap. While insurance companies are known for their funny ads—like Jake from State Farm or Flo from Progressive—the real takeaway isn't just the laughs. These campaigns often remind us how important it is to actually have insurance when the unexpected happens. You've probably seen a TV show or movie where someone crashes and yells, "Damn! I didn't opt for the insurance." It's funny on screen, but in real life, not having coverage can be a costly mistake. We're going to cover what insurance is and the various types available to help you determine which ones are best for you at any given time, *just in case.*

45 Chris Rock, Bigger and Blacker, television comedy special, directed by Keith Truesdell, aired July 10, 1999, on HBO.

Q&A SESSION

What's Insurance, and How Does It Work?

According to Investopedia, insurance is basically a contract—called a **policy**—between you and an insurance company that provides financial protection when something goes wrong.[46] In simple terms, you pay a company to help cover the cost of unexpected losses, whether it's car damage, hospital bills, or even theft. Many different types of insurance are available; these are the most common policy types for people in the US:

- Auto insurance (which is required by law in most states)
- Health insurance
- Homeowner's or renter's insurance
- Life insurance

Most people carry at least one of these, if not more. Insurance isn't just for individuals—businesses need it too. For example, a fast-food restaurant might have coverage for injuries if a worker gets burned while frying food. Hospitals often carry malpractice insurance in case of lawsuits over patient care. Some companies even bring in brokers to manage the different insurance needs of their staff. And depending on the state, businesses may be legally required to carry certain types of coverage. Specialized policies like these are also available:

- Kidnap and ransom insurance
- Identity theft coverage
- Wedding insurance (yes, that's a real thing)

46 Julia Kagan, "What Is Insurance?," Investopedia, May 8, 2025, https://www.investopedia.com/terms/i/insurance.asp.

At the end of the day, insurance is about managing financial risk. If something bad happens, and you don't have coverage, you'll pay the full cost out of your pocket. But with the right policy, the insurance company steps in to cover some or all the expenses depending on what's included in your plan. Insurance can help protect your health, income, family, and peace of mind.

Insurance policies have several components:[47]

Premium. A policy's **premium** is just a fancy way of saying the cost of the insurance—usually paid monthly. But that price isn't one size fits all. Insurance companies look at your level of risk to decide how much you'll pay. In other words, the more likely you are to file a claim, the more they'll charge you. Let's say you own a few luxury cars and have a history of speeding tickets. You'll likely pay more for auto insurance compared to someone who drives a basic sedan and has a clean record. These factors are examples of what affects your premiums for different types of policies:

- Auto insurance. Your driving history, past claims, age, where you live, and even your credit score can all influence the cost.
- Home insurance. This depends on the value of your home, the amount of coverage, your claims history, and your location.
- Health insurance. Things like your age, gender, where you live, and your health can all affect your monthly cost.
- Life insurance. Here they look at your age, gender, tobacco use, overall health, and how much coverage you want.

The bottom line—insurance companies charge based on how much of a risk you appear to be. So the less risky you seem, the lower your premiums might be.

47 Kagan, "What Is Insurance?"

Policy limit. A **policy limit** is the maximum amount your insurance company will pay for a covered claim. This limit might apply to each incident, each year or policy term, or even over your entire lifetime, depending on the type of insurance. The higher the coverage limit, the more you'll usually pay in premiums. For example, with life insurance, the policy limit is often called the **face value**—that's the amount your beneficiary will receive when you pass away. For health insurance, things work a bit differently. Thanks to the Affordable Care Act (ACA), insurance companies are not allowed to set lifetime limits on essential health services, like maternity care, family planning, or pediatric services. This means there's no cap on what your plan can cover for these benefits while your policy is active.[48]

Figure 4.1 illustrates three types of insurance policy limits by showing their corresponding coverage amounts in dollars:

1. Per Incident Limit
   - Coverage: $10,000
   - This is the maximum amount the policy will pay for a *single* event or claim.
   - For example, if you go to the emergency room once, this is the most your insurance would cover for that one visit.
2. Annual Limit
   - Coverage: $50,000
   - This is the maximum the policy will pay *within a single year*, regardless of how many incidents occur. For example, if you have multiple claims in one year, the total coverage can't exceed this amount.
3. Lifetime Limit

48 U.S. Department of Health and Human Services, "About the Affordable Care Act," accessed August 14, 2025, https://www.hhs.gov/healthcare/about-the-aca/index.html.

- Coverage: $200,000
- This is the **total cap** on benefits the policy will ever pay over the *entire lifetime* of the policy.
- Once you hit this amount, the policy will not cover any additional expenses.

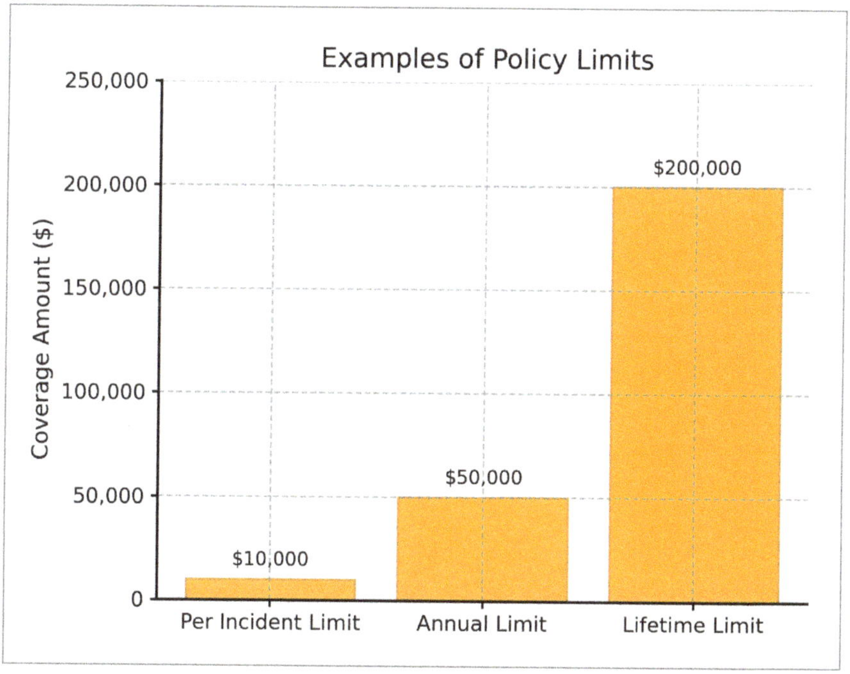

Figure 4.1 Source: Your Blueprint for Financial Literacy

Deductible. A **deductible** is the amount you pay out of your own pocket before your insurance company starts covering the rest. Deductibles are designed to cut down on small claims and to make sure people don't file for every little thing. Here's a simple example: Let's say your car gets damaged and the repair cost is $2,000. If your deductible is $1,000, you'll pay that first thousand, and the insurance company will cover the rest.

Deductibles can work differently depending on the type of policy. Some apply per claim, while others apply per year—like in health insurance, where you might have a separate individual and family deductible. In general, the higher the deductible, the lower your monthly premium tends to be. That's because you agree to pay more out of pocket if something happens—you're less likely to file small claims. Most people are familiar with deductibles when it comes to things like doctor visits or car repairs. Figure 4.2, "How Deductibles Affect Insurance Premiums," explains the inverse relationship between deductible amounts and monthly premium costs in an insurance policy.

What This Means for You

- Choosing a *higher deductible* can save you money on your *monthly premium*, but you'll pay *more out of pocket* if you need to file a claim.
- However, a *lower deductible* costs *more monthly* but offers *more financial protection* when something happens.

You're paying less each month when you agree to cover more out-of-pocket costs through a higher deductible. This is a trade-off. Figure 4.2 explains:

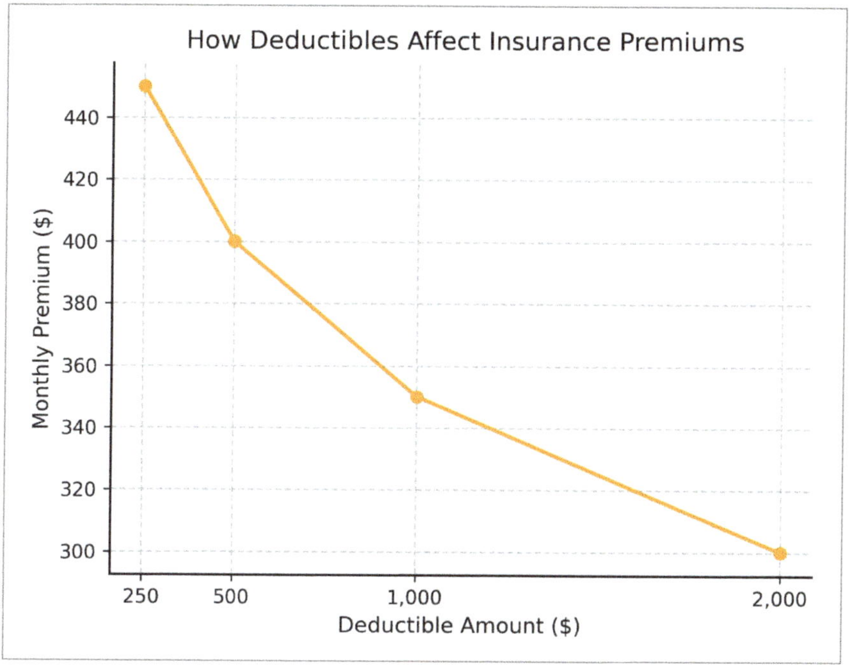

Figure 4.2 Source: Your Blueprint for Financial Literacy

What's Life Insurance?

Life insurance is a policy that provides financial support to your loved ones if you pass away. In exchange for paying a regular premium, the insurance company promises to pay a lump sum to the people you name as beneficiaries—like your spouse or children.[49]

There are two main types of life insurance:[50]

Term life insurance covers you for a set number of years—like ten, twenty, or thirty. If you die during that time, your loved ones get paid. But if the term ends and you're still alive, the coverage stops unless you renew or convert it.

Permanent life insurance (or **whole life**) covers you for your entire life as long as you keep up with the payments. It also builds

49 Pat Howard, "Life Insurance: What It Is, How It Works, and How to Buy a Policy," Investopedia, May 8, 2025, https://www.investopedia.com/terms/l/lifeinsurance.asp.

50 Howard, "Life Insurance: What It Is, How It Works, and How to Buy a Policy."

cash value over time that you can sometimes borrow from. Listed below are some common types of permanent life insurance:

- **Whole life insurance.** Permanent coverage with a savings (cash value) portion that grows at a fixed rate set by the insurer.
- **Universal life (UL).** Permanent policy with interest-earning cash value and flexible premiums/death benefits that can be adjusted over time.
- **Variable life.** Permanent policy where cash value can be invested (often in mutual funds); growth potential is higher but carries investment risk.
- **Variable universal life (VUL).** Combines flexible premiums of UL with investment choices of Variable Life; returns depend on market performance.
- **Indexed universal life (IUL).** Cash value growth tied to a stock index (e.g., S&P 500); includes caps on gains, floors against losses, and flexible premiums.
- **Final expense insurance.** A smaller whole life policy designed to cover funeral and burial costs; usually more affordable.
- **Simplified issue life insurance.** No medical exam required; quicker approval but usually higher premiums. Available in term, whole, or universal versions.
- **Guaranteed issue life insurance.** No health questions or exams; accessible for people with health issues, but offers lower benefits and higher premiums.

Common Life Insurance Riders

Riders are optional add-ons you can attach to a life insurance policy.

They provide extra protection or flexibility but usually increase the cost. Here are some of the most common riders:

- **Accidental death benefit (ADB) rider.** Adds an extra payout if death is caused by an accident.
  Drawback: Only applies in the event of an accident.
- **Waiver of premium rider.** Waives premium payments if you become disabled and can't work.
  Drawback: Disability must meet strict policy definitions.
- **Long-term care rider.** Lets you use part of the death benefit to pay for long-term care expenses.
  Drawback: Reduces the death benefit available to beneficiaries.
- **Guaranteed insurability rider.** Allows you to buy more coverage later without another medical exam.
  Drawback: Usually limited to certain times or coverage amounts.
- **Child term rider.** Provides temporary life insurance for children until they reach a set age.
  Drawback: Coverage ends once the child reaches that age.
- **Return of premium rider.** Refunds all or part of your premiums if you outlive your term policy.
  Drawback: Comes with much higher premiums.
- **Chronic illness rider.** Gives access to part of the death benefit if you're diagnosed with a chronic illness.
  Drawback: Reduces the remaining death benefit if used early.

I once heard a joke where someone asked a man why he didn't have life insurance. He said, "Because when I die, I want it to be a sad day for everybody." It's funny—but in real life, life insurance can give your family peace of mind during a hard time. If you're looking for something long term, I highly suggest taking a closer look at permanent or whole life insurance. Table 4.1 compares term life and permanent life insurance in simple terms:

Feature	Term Life	Permanent Life
Coverage Duration	10–30 years	Lifetime
Monthly Cost	Lower	Higher
Builds Cash Value	No	Yes
Expires After Term	Yes	No
Can Be Borrowed Against	No	Yes
Best For	Short-term needs, young families	Lifelong coverage, estate planning

Table 4.1 Source: Your Blueprint for Financial Literacy

What's Home Insurance?

Homeowner's insurance is designed to protect your house, your belongings, and any additional structures on your property, like a garage or shed. Your homeowner's policy can cover events like fire, theft, vandalism, and certain types of accidental damage. However, it typically doesn't cover floods or earthquakes—those require separate policies. If you need extra protection for high-value items or specific situations, you can add **riders** to your policy. As stated earlier, riders are add-ons to your policy that give you extra coverage for something not included in the basic plan, though these come at an additional cost.[51]

Renter's insurance works in a similar way but focuses on protecting your personal belongings if you rent rather than own your

51 Eric Estevez, "What Is Homeowners Insurance and How Does It Work?," Investopedia, March 5, 2024, https://www.investopedia.com/terms/h/homeowners-insurance.asp.

home. The policy won't cover the building itself—that's the property manager's responsibility but it will help replace your things if there's a fire, water damage, or a break-in.

I've had friends and neighbors go through this—and let's just say, Jake from State Farm never showed up. If you have a mortgage, your lender will almost always require you to carry homeowner's insurance. And if you cancel your policy or stop paying, the lender can take out a policy on your behalf—and yes, it'll probably be more expensive than if you'd just kept your own. Even if you're renting, having coverage is smart. Imagine coming home to find everything damaged or destroyed and realizing nothing's covered.

What's Auto Insurance?

Auto insurance is designed to help cover the cost of damage or injury caused by a car accident. It can also help pay for repairs if your car is stolen, vandalized, or damaged by weather, like hail or flooding. Instead of paying these costs entirely out of pocket, you pay a yearly premium to your insurance company, and if something happens, they step in to cover most or all of the approved expenses.[52] If you're financing or leasing a car, your lender or dealership will usually require you to carry auto insurance. If you don't, they may buy a policy for you and add the cost to your loan—and let's be honest, that's almost always more expensive.

Just like with home insurance, your car insurance premium is based on several personal and vehicle-related factors. These can vary depending on the type of coverage you choose, but common pricing factors include the following:

- Your driving history (tickets, accidents, or claims)
- Your age, location, and credit score

52 Julia Kagan, "Understanding Auto Insurance: Coverage, Costs, and How It Works," Investopedia, updated November 10, 2025, https://www.investopedia.com/terms/a/auto-insurance.asp.

- The make, model, and year of your vehicle
- The ownership status, whether the car is leased, financed, or owned outright

How to buy insurance for a new car. Before you can drive off the lot with your new car, you'll need proof of insurance. Dealerships typically won't release the keys until you show coverage. Here's what to know:[53]

- **Already insured?** Call your current insurance company before or during the purchase. They can update your policy to include the new car and tell you how your premium will change.
- **Grace periods may apply.** Some policies temporarily cover a new car for a few days, but don't rely on it. Always add the car to your policy as soon as possible.
- **No insurance yet?** Shop around before buying. Compare multiple quotes, not only for price but also coverage limits and discounts. Cars with advanced safety systems or anti-theft features often qualify for reduced rates.
- **Required information.** When contacting an insurer, be ready with this information:
    - Driver's license (yours and any other drivers on the policy)
    - Vehicle identification number (VIN)
    - Odometer reading
    - Vehicle details (make, model, year, and trim level)
    - Safety or anti-theft features (airbags, cameras, alarms, etc.)

53 Drew Gula, "The 5 Best Car Insurance Companies of August 2025," NerdWallet, accessed August 25, 2025, https://www.nerdwallet.com/best/insurance/car-insurance-new-car.

- Loan or lease details (if financing or leasing).
- Current policy already has insurance, for comparison

Key takeaway: No proof of insurance means no car. Make sure coverage is in place before leaving the dealership.

Having this information ready will speed up the process, help you get accurate quotes, and get you on the road faster.

Collision and comprehensive insurance. When people talk about full-coverage auto insurance, they're usually referring to a combination of collision and comprehensive coverage. These two types of protection work differently, and it's good to know what each one covers.[54] **Collision insurance** pays for repairs to your car if you crash into another vehicle or object, like a guardrail or traffic pole, or even if another car hits you. **Comprehensive insurance**[55] covers no collision damage—things like theft, fire, vandalism, or natural disasters (like floods or hailstorms). Your premium for these coverages depends on several factors:

- Your driving history and claims record
- The type of car you drive
- Your deductible amount
- Your coverage limits

Let me share a quick story: I once got hit by a truck pulling a U-Haul trailer. The driver cut in front of me and sideswiped my car with the trailer. At first, it didn't seem serious, so we just exchanged information. Big mistake! Turns out, the guy had a fake license, and the insurance company couldn't find him. From that point

54 Julia Kagan, "Collision Insurance: What It Is, How It Works," Investopedia, last modified March 7, 2024, https://www.investopedia.com/terms/c/collision-insurance.asp.

55 Julia Kagan, "What Is Comprehensive Insurance and What Does It Cover?," Investopedia, July 19, 2024, https://www.investopedia.com/terms/c/comprehensive-insurance.asp.

on, I learned the hard way—always call the police when you're in an accident, even if it doesn't seem major.

Personal liability insurance. Personal liability insurance is part of your auto insurance policy and helps protect you if you cause an accident. It covers two key things:[56]

- Bodily injury in case someone else gets hurt
- Property damage in case their car or other property is damaged

This type of coverage is *required* in most states, and it's one of the most important parts of your auto insurance. If you're found at fault in an accident, this is the coverage that steps in to help pay for *the other party's* medical bills and repairs. Your premium for liability coverage depends on several things, including these factors:

- Your driving record
- Your age and credit score
- Your history of claims
- Your location

If you've had at-fault accidents or have filed multiple claims, your insurance company may view you as a higher risk and charge you more. Also, some states have higher minimum-coverage limits, which can raise the cost of your policy. Even though it's required, the amount of liability coverage you choose can go above your state's minimum requirements—and that's often a smart move for better protection.

56 Ryan Brady, "Liability Car Insurance: What It Covers and How Much You Need," NerdWallet, March 28, 2024, https://www.nerdwallet.com/article/insurance/auto/liability-car-insurance.

Uninsured or underinsured motorist insurance. Some states require drivers to carry **uninsured** or **underinsured motorist coverage** as part of their auto insurance policy. This type of coverage protects you in situations where the other driver doesn't have insurance, doesn't have enough of it, or leaves the scene—like in a hit-and-run.[57] Even though car insurance is required in most states, not everyone follows the rules. Some areas have a higher number of uninsured drivers, and if you live in one of those areas, you could end up paying more for this coverage. The cost of this protection also depends on the coverage limits you choose. The higher your limits, the more it may cost—but it can also give you better financial protection if something serious happens. This type of coverage is one of those things you hope you never need, but you'll be glad to have it if you do.

How to save money on car insurance for a new car. People often ask *Is it cheaper to insure a new car?* In most cases, the answer is no. New vehicles usually cost more to insure than used ones, mainly because they have a higher value and can cost more to repair or replace. That said, you can cut down your insurance costs in several ways, even with a brand-new car. Use these tips to help you save:[58]

- Ask about discounts. Many insurance companies offer discounts for things like a good driving history, bundled policies (auto and home), low mileage, or even certain safety features in your car.
- Raise your deductible. Increasing your deductible can lower your premium. Make sure it's an amount you can actually afford to pay out of pocket if something happens.

57 Andrew Marder, "What Is Uninsured Motorist Coverage?," NerdWallet, June 8, 2023, https://www.nerdwallet.com/article/insurance/uninsured-motorist-coverage.

58 Daniel Myers, "Bundle Your Insurance for Big Savings," Investopedia, January 23, 2022, https://www.investopedia.com/articles/insurance/09/bundle-insurance.asp.

- Compare quotes. Don't just go with the first offer. Shop around and compare quotes from different companies.
- Maintain good credit. Believe it or not, your credit score can affect your rate. A better score often leads to a better premium.
- Drive safely. Tickets and accidents can raise your rates. The longer you go without a claim, the more potential you have to qualify for a lower premium.
- Choose the right vehicle. Cars with strong safety ratings, anti-theft systems, and lower repair costs are usually cheaper to insure.

Are you starting to see how different subjects are related and dependent on each other?

What's Health Insurance?

Health insurance is designed to help with the cost of medical care—whether it's for routine checkups or unexpected emergencies. You can also choose to add vision and dental coverage, but those usually come as separate plans. Most health insurance plans include an annual deductible. That's what you pay out of pocket before your coverage kicks in. After that, you might still have to cover **copays** (flat fees) and **coinsurance** (a percentage of the bill).[59]

But the good news is that many preventive services, like annual physicals or screenings, are covered at no cost, even before you meet your deductible. There are several ways to obtain health insurance:[60]

Option 1. Use the government's Health Insurance Marketplace. The Health Insurance Marketplace—sometimes called the healthcare exchange—is one way you can shop for a health

59 Julia Kagan, "Health Insurance: Definition, How It Works," Investopedia, last modified May 29, 2024, https://www.investopedia.com/terms/h/healthinsurance.asp.

60 Amy Fontinelle, "How to Get Health Insurance?," Investopedia, February 7, 2023, https://www.investopedia.com/how-to-get-health-insurance-4772855.

insurance plan. Depending on your income and whether you have other options (like coverage through your job), you might qualify for financial assistance, known as premium tax credits or subsidies. Even if you're eligible for health insurance through your employer, it doesn't hurt to check the Marketplace. You might find a better or more affordable plan that works for you. Keep in mind that if your employer coverage is considered affordable and meets minimum standards, you probably won't qualify for a subsidy.

You'll need to enroll during the annual open enrollment period—unless you have a qualifying life event, like getting married, having a baby, or moving to a new state. If you miss the window and don't qualify for a special enrollment, you'll have to wait until the next open enrollment period to get coverage. You can apply through these methods:

- Via HealthCare.gov
- By phone
- In person with help from a certified application counselor or Marketplace navigator (many states have these available)

To use the Marketplace, you must have US citizenship or a lawful presence in the country. Just go to HealthCare.gov and enter your ZIP code, then the page will direct you to either the federal site or your state's Marketplace, if your state runs its own.

Option 2. Work with an agent or broker. Another way to get health insurance is by working with a licensed insurance agent or broker. These professionals know the ins and outs of health plans and can help you compare options based on your specific needs.

You can find someone qualified through the federal government's Find Local Help tool. To keep your options open, it's a good idea to work with a broker who sells both Marketplace and non-Marketplace plans. That way you'll see a broader range of choices—and you're more likely to get unbiased guidance. Here's the difference between agents and brokers:

- An **agent** usually represents one insurance company.
- A **broker** works with several companies and can offer more plan options.

One important thing to know—you don't pay brokers directly, and working with one doesn't increase your premium. Insurance companies pay them a commission when they help you enroll, so there's no extra cost to you. Some brokers also show plans on private enrollment sites, but if you want to qualify for government subsidies, you'll need to apply through HealthCare.gov or your state exchange.

Option 3. Buy directly from an insurance company. Not every health plan is listed on the Health Insurance Marketplace. Sometimes, you might find a policy that better fits your budget or needs by going directly to an insurance company's website. Remember, though, when you shop this way, you're only seeing options from that one company, so you'll need to check multiple sites to compare. Plans sold outside the Marketplace still have to follow **ACA** rules if they're ACA-compliant. This means they must

- cover pre-existing conditions,
- offer essential health benefits, and
- provide free preventive care before you meet your deductible.

Yes, these protections came from the ACA, also known as Obamacare, introduced under President Barack Obama. There are also short-term plans you can buy outside the Marketplace. These usually last up to twelve months and have lower monthly premiums but less coverage. Most won't cover pre-existing conditions, and they often exclude important benefits like prescription drugs, mental health care, or maternity coverage.

So, although the price looks good, you could be left with huge bills if something serious happens. These plans are often marketed as a just-in-case option, especially if you're between jobs, but be sure to read the fine print. Cheaper doesn't always mean better. Also, keep this in mind: If you don't buy your plan through the Marketplace, you won't qualify for subsidies—even if your income drops later. That could mean missing out on real savings just because you didn't go through the right channel.

Option 4. Buy through an online health insurance brokerage. Online brokerages—also called **private exchanges**—let you compare health insurance plans and apply for coverage online. While these sites can be helpful, it's important to know that they usually only show plans that will earn them a **commission** if you sign up. Some plans might even be highlighted simply because they pay the site more money, not necessarily because they're better for you. That doesn't mean the plans are bad—but you may not be seeing every available option that fits your needs. Also, unlike the official state or federal marketplaces, these sites may ask for *additional* personal information like your height, weight, or pre-existing conditions. The sites can use that information to market other products to you or to share it with their business partners. And just like when you buy directly from an insurance company, you *won't qualify* for subsidies if you use a private exchange. So before enrolling, make sure you understand what you're being shown—and *what you might be missing.*

Option 5. Buy through a membership organization. If you're part of a union, alumni group, freelancers' network, or professional association, you might be able to get group health insurance through it. For example, the Freelancers Union offers plans through its partners, like HealthPlan Services. Group plans may offer better rates than buying a policy on your own—but be sure to read the fine print. Some associations only offer **discount plans**, not actual insurance. A discount plan might help with glasses or prescriptions, but it won't do much if you're facing something serious like cancer or surgery. And even if the organization is a nonprofit, the insurance itself may be sold through a for-profit partner. Treat it like any other insurance purchase—read, compare, and ask questions. As you've probably gathered by now, if your job doesn't offer health insurance, you've still got plenty of ways to find coverage; you just need to know where to look.

What's Umbrella Insurance?

Umbrella insurance is additional liability coverage that kicks in after your regular auto, home, or watercraft policy limits are maxed out. You can't buy it on its own; you'll need to have a base policy first. This type of coverage is especially helpful if you own valuable assets, engage in higher-risk activities, or simply want added peace of mind.

Even small-business owners use it as a backup in case they get sued. Premiums are usually lower if you bundle with your current insurer. Some providers may require that you carry at least $150,000–$250,000 in auto coverage and $250,000–$300,000 in home coverage before adding umbrella protection. Umbrella insurance—also known as **excess liability insurance**—helps cover legal costs and damages that go beyond your regular coverage so you don't have to dip into savings or assets.[61] As a rental property owner, I've found it useful—plus, it was tax deductible.

What's Travel Insurance?

Travel insurance—for the trips that don't go as planned. Travel insurance can be a real lifesaver when things don't go smoothly, whether it's bad weather delaying your flight or an unexpected injury during your vacation. Some premium travel credit cards

61 Julia Kagan, "What Is an Umbrella Insurance Policy? Definition and Who Needs It," Investopedia, updated January 26, 2024, https://www.investopedia.com/terms/u/umbrella-insurance-policy.asp

include limited coverage, but you can also buy a plan directly from a private insurer. Policies vary by provider and even by state. You should know about these key types of travel insurance:[62]

- **Trip cancellation and trip interruption.** Trip cancellation helps cover the cost of *prepaid, nonrefundable expenses*—like flights or hotels—if you must cancel before your trip due to a covered reason, such as jury duty, losing your job, or a major storm. Trip interruption applies *once your trip has started* and helps you recover some costs if you must cut your trip short unexpectedly.
- **Cancel for any reason.** This is an optional upgrade that lets you cancel your trip for literally any reason and still receive a partial refund. You'll need to cancel at least *two days before your departure*, and not all policies offer this option, so check before you buy.
- **Travel medical insurance.** This type of policy is focused on emergency medical care while you're abroad. It usually includes emergency treatment, medical evacuation or repatriation, accidental death coverage, and 24/7 travel assistance. Travel medical insurance is typically more affordable than full coverage because it doesn't include trip cancellation or delay protections.

What Are the Benefits of Buying More Insurance with One Insurer?

Bundling insurance policies can save you money. According to Investopedia, big-name insurance companies often design their pricing strategies to attract a certain type of customer—usually someone who needs more than just car insurance. They're looking

62 Benajmin Din, "How to Find the Best Travel Insurance," NerdWallet, updated January 21, 2026, https://www.nerdwallet.com/travel/learn/travel-insurance.

for people who also want to insure their home, life, or even other assets—folks who are likely to stick around for a while instead of shopping for a cheaper deal every six months. That's why many of these companies offer **multipolicy** (or **bundling**) **discounts**. In short, the more policies you buy from the same company, the more money you may save.[63]

While another company might beat them on price for one type of insurance—like car coverage—those savings often don't hold up once you factor in the discounts you'd get by bundling your home, auto, and life insurance together with a single provider. Plus, realistically, managing one bill and one company is much easier than trying to juggle multiple policies from different places. So bundling your insurance doesn't just save you money; it can save you time and hassle too.

63 Myers, "Bundle Your Insurance for Big Savings."

CHAPTER 4 TAKEAWAYS

You should now have a better understanding of the following:

- ✓ **Fundamentals of insurance.** Understanding the basics of insurance—like what it's for and the different types out there—can help you sort through your options and figure out which coverage makes the most sense for you.
- ✓ **Protection awareness.** Knowing when and why to obtain various insurances (life, home, auto, health, umbrella, or travel) will help you protect yourself and your assets.
- ✓ **Buying strategies.** Guidance on how to purchase insurance and the advantages of bundling policies will help you make cost-effective decisions.

Source: Your Blueprint for Financial Literacy

Chapter 5

How Do I Buy a Home?

When it comes to buying a home, don't just fall in love with the look—know what you can handle. Out of all the major decisions you'll face in life, I'd argue this one is near the top for most people in the US: Should I buy a home? We've all heard this before: "Owning a home is the American dream." But here's something I've learned: When you step into this kind of commitment, aim to buy a *home*, not just a *house*.

A home is a place where memories are made—where your friends and family feel welcomed. A house, however, can easily become something you buy to impress people rather than to meet your actual needs. And not knowing the difference can lead to buying beyond your budget and in some cases, foreclosure.

I've seen people walk through a property and say things like *My mom would love this* or *This will wow my friends.* That's your first sign they're buying based on someone else's taste, not their own lifestyle or financial situation. If you're single with a steady income, be honest with yourself: Do you really need five bedrooms and bathrooms? Or are you thinking about how good it'll look to others? What you buy should be rightsized for your life and your wallet—*not your ego.* It's okay if now isn't your time to buy. Maybe you'll need to rent for a bit while you save and plan. That's not a setback—that's called being smart with your finances.

Here are some common things people consider when buying a home:

- Will it fit my current or future family needs?
- Should I choose a fifteen- or thirty-year mortgage?
- Is it close to highways or public transportation?
- Is it in a quiet area, or is the location noisy?
- How much can I actually afford?
- Is the home in a flood zone?
- What are the schools like in the area?

Of course, plenty of other questions might come up, but these are some of the most common. Buying a home is likely one of the biggest purchases you'll ever make, so take your time. Do your research. And remember, don't let your eyes—or your ego—be bigger than your bank account.

Q&A SESSION

Where Do I Start?

There are tons of ways to begin your home-buying journey but let me tell you where mine started. It was 2007, and my wife, Zenaye, and I had just moved from London to New York City. All over the news, one phrase kept repeating like a broken record: *subprime mortgage*. You couldn't turn on the TV or radio without hearing it. And the stories were heartbreaking—people were losing their homes, jobs, and life savings. The subprime meltdown began around 2007 when a large number of risky home loans, given to people with poor credit, started going into default. During the housing boom of the early 2000s, lenders approved more of these high-risk loans because interest rates were low and demand for homes was high. But when the housing market crashed, many borrowers couldn't keep up with their payments. This wave of defaults triggered the financial crisis and the Great Recession.[64] I'd never bought a home before, but I wanted to learn fast. So, I went to Barnes & Noble and picked up a copy of *The Complete Idiot's Guide to Buying a Home*. Best. Decision. Ever. It broke things down in a way that actually made sense. I even turned what I learned into a PowerPoint presentation and sent it to friends and family to help them also get a better understanding, which eventually led to me writing this book. Nowadays, you don't even have to leave your house to get solid guidance on home buying. One of the best online tools I've found is from the US Department of Housing and Urban Development. It walks you through the entire home-buying process step-by-step.[65] One of the most important sections on the site is "Know Your Rights," which includes information on these topics:

- Fair housing
- The Real Estate Settlement Procedures Act
- Borrower's rights
- Warnings about predatory lending

This is your future home we're talking about. It pays to be informed before you sign anything.

Why Do I Need a Down Payment?

A **down payment** is the up-front amount you pay when buying something big—like a house or a car.[66] It's usually a percentage of the total cost, and the rest is financed through a loan. The more money you put down, the less you borrow, the less interest you'll pay, and the

64 Jill Kenton, "Subprime Meltdown: What Was It, What Happened, Consequences?," Investopedia, updated September 10, 2024, https://www.investopedia.com/terms/s/subprime-meltdown.asp.

65 U.S. Department of Housing and Urban Development, "Buying a Home," Helping Americans, accessed July 23, 2025, https://www.hud.gov/helping-americans/buying-a-home.

66 Investopedia Team, "Down Payment: What It Is and How Much Is Required," Investopedia. August 26, 2024, https://www.investopedia.com/terms/d/down_payment.asp.

lower your monthly payments will be. People often use *down payment* and *deposit* interchangeably. When it comes to buying a home, most first-time buyers put down about 6% of the home's price. As of 2023, conventional loans required as little as 3% down, and Federal Housing Administration loans needed at least 3.5%.[67]

Lower down payments may come with income limits and higher fees depending on your credit scores. Yes, we're talking about credit scores again! Here's why a bigger down payment can help:[68]

- **Save on interest.** Borrowing $100,000 at 5% equals $93,256 in total interest over thirty years. But borrowing $80,000 instead (after a $20,000 down payment) saves nearly $20,000 in interest.
- **Lower your monthly payments.** You can lower your monthly payments. For the $100,000 loan, your monthly payment would be $537, but with the $80,000 loan, you'd pay $429 per month.
- **Avoid private mortgage insurance.** If you put down less than 20%, most lenders require private mortgage insurance. This protects them—not you—if you stop making payments. Once you've built up 20% equity, you can ask the lender to remove the private mortgage insurance.

Down payments show lenders you're serious about the loan. If you can't put down a large amount right away, consider making extra payments on your mortgage each month—this strategy is called **accelerated amortization** and can save you money long term.

If your finances improve after you get the initial mortgage, you can even **refinance** and apply a larger down payment to the new loan. I refinanced an investment property with a different lender,

67 Andrew Dehan, "What Is a Conventional Loan?," Bankrate, July 10, 2025, https://www.bankrate.com/mortgages/what-is-a-conventional-loan.

68 Investopedia Team, "Down Payment: What It Is and How Much Is Required."

and my interest rates went from 5% to 3.4% during the COVID pandemic when the interest rates dropped. This saved me loads of money that I could put toward the principal, allowing me to pay for the property sooner with a lot less interest. Remember APY works for the lender, not you. Refer to table 5.1 to compare down payments.

Table 5.1. Down Payment Comparison

Down Payment	Loan Amount	Monthly Payment (5% Interest)	Total Interest over 30 Years
$0 (100% Loan)	$100,000	$537	$93,256
$10,000 (10%)	$90,000	$483	$83,930
$20,000 (20%)	$80,000	$429	$74,605

Table 5.1 Source: Your Blueprint for Financial Literacy

What's a Mortgage, and How Do I Choose the Best One for Me?

A **mortgage** is a type of loan people use to buy or refinance real estate, usually homes.[69] You agree to repay the loan over time through regular payments, which include both the original loan amount (the principal) and interest. What makes a mortgage unique is that your home becomes the lender's **security**—if you stop paying, they can take your home through **foreclosure**. You don't have to pay the full price of a home up front. Most folks put down a percentage (a down payment), and the mortgage covers the rest. This is how many people in the US afford homeownership. For example, if a home costs $300,000, you might put down $60,000 (20%) and borrow the remaining $240,000.

To get a mortgage, you'll need to apply through a lender, like a bank or credit union. They'll check things like your income, debt, credit score, and job stability. Your mortgage will also have

69 Julia Kagan, "What Is a Mortgage? Types, How They Work, and Examples," Investopedia, July 19, 2024, https://www.investopedia.com/terms/m/mortgage.asp.

a specific term—usually fifteen or thirty years. Most are fixed rate, meaning the interest rate stays the same. Others, like adjustable-rate mortgages, have interest rates that can change over time. If you're approved, the process ends with a **closing**, the day you pay the down payment, sign the papers, and officially become the homeowner. Some lenders may charge fees at closing, including loan origination fees and points, which are upfront charges that may reduce the loan's interest rate.

There are several types of mortgages:[70]

- **Fixed rate** is the most traditional kind. Your interest rate and monthly payments stay the same for the life of the loan.
- **Adjustable-rate mortgages** start off with a lower rate for a set time, then the rate adjusts periodically. They're good for the short term but risky if rates rise.
- With **interest-only mortgages**, you pay only interest for a certain period before the loan converts to a regular payment schedule. These can be risky and are best for people who really understand them.
- **Reverse mortgages** are available to homeowners ages sixty-two and older. A reverse mortgage lets you borrow against your home's equity. You receive money in different forms, and repayment happens when you move, sell, or pass away.
- **Government-backed** loans from the Federal Housing Administration (FHA), Veterans Administration (VA), and US Department of Agriculture (USDA) help people who may not qualify for conventional loans due to income or credit challenges.

70 Kagan, "What Is a Mortgage? Types, How They Work, and Examples."

A mortgage can be a powerful tool—if managed wisely. Always read the fine print, ask questions, and make sure the monthly payment fits your budget. And remember, just because a bank approves you for a certain amount does not mean you should spend it all. Your wallet, not your ego, should always have the final say.

Bonus tip—you can lower your mortgage interest rate by buying points up front, but this only makes sense if you plan to stay in the home long enough to benefit. Otherwise, that money might be better spent elsewhere. And if anyone ever tries to rush you into a mortgage you don't understand, remember that it's your home and your money. Move at your own pace.

What's a Cosigner, and Will I Need One?

A cosigner can be anyone who promises to take on the responsibilities of paying the loan if the other signer defaults. Cosigning a mortgage is a big deal—so big that I usually see only parents or close family members step into this role.[71] This isn't merely a kind gesture; it's a legally binding financial promise. Often, the borrower doesn't earn enough or has a high debt-to-income ratio, which makes it hard to qualify for a loan on their own. A cosigner's income or assets can help, but remember, their credit won't always boost the application. In fact, lenders may consider the lowest credit score of all parties involved. Also, unlike co-borrowers, cosigners don't own any part of the property. They're only there to back up the borrower financially.

If you cosign and the borrower misses payments, here's what could happen:[72]

- Your credit score could take a hit.
- Late fees could fall on you.

71 Chase Bank, "Co-Signing for a Mortgage: What Borrowers and Co-Signers Need to Know," Accessed July 23, 2025, https://www.chase.com/personal/mortgage/education/financing-a-home/cosigning-a-mortgage-loan.

72 Chase, "Co-Signing for a Mortgage: What Borrowers and Co-Signers Need to Know."

- Foreclosure could end up on your credit report.
- Your ability to borrow in the future could be affected.
- Your own debt-to-income ratio would increase.

Before agreeing, you'll need to provide personal and financial documents just like the borrower will:

- Identification. You'll need to show proof of your identity, address, and Social Security number.
- Financial records. Lenders will need to see your tax returns, W-2s, pay stubs, account statements, investment balances, and a credit check.
- Proof of relationship. Some lenders may require that you're closely related to the borrower, especially for certain loan programs.

If the borrower pays on time, you might forget you ever cosigned. But if they miss payments, your credit could suffer. A single missed mortgage payment can drop your credit score, potentially raising your interest rates on other loans. Plus, this new obligation can affect your ability to borrow money for your own home, car, or anything else.

Here's a helpful tip: Your name won't appear on the title if you're only a cosigner. You're simply guaranteeing the loan. Getting out of the agreement isn't easy either. Typically, the borrower would have to refinance the loan without your income to remove your name.

If cosigning isn't ideal, there are alternatives. Some homebuyers qualify for government-backed loans, like FHA or VA loans, or down payment–assistance programs through state housing agencies. In many cases, a family member or loved one might consider giving money toward a down payment rather than cosigning. That way, they avoid taking on debt but still provide meaningful support.[73]

Before agreeing to cosign, consider speaking with a home-lending advisor to explore all the borrower's options. There may be a path forward that doesn't put your credit or finances at risk.

Do I Use a Bank or a Mortgage Company to Borrow Money?

To be honest, this question doesn't come up often, but it should. Understanding the difference between getting a mortgage through a traditional bank versus a mortgage company can save you time and money. According to SmartAsset, full-service banks are federally chartered institutions that offer mortgage loans along with checking and savings accounts, business loans, and even investment products. They're regulated by the FDIC. Mortgage companies, however, are regulated by individual states and focus solely on home loans. While mortgage companies don't offer other financial services, they can often move faster and have more flexible loan options.[74]

Mortgage Options: Banks versus Mortgage Companies:

Getting a Mortgage Through a Bank

Pros

- Banks may offer existing customers special benefits, like lower interest rates or exclusive loan programs.
- Most banks service the loans they originate, so you continue dealing with the same bank for monthly payments, which can be convenient.

73 Chase, "Co-Signing for a Mortgage: What Borrowers and Co-Signers Need to Know."

74 Gregory Erich Phillips, "Should I Get a Loan Through a Mortgage Company or Bank?," SmartAsset, updated October 28, 2025, https://smartasset.com/mortgage/should-i-get-my-loan-through-a-mortgage-company-or-a-bank.

Cons

- Lending standards are typically stricter due to federal compliance requirements.

Getting a Mortgage Through a Mortgage Company

Pros

- They may offer a wider range of loan products compared to banks.
- Mortgage companies can often close loans faster because they focus solely on mortgages.
- Faster closings mean you may benefit from shorter rate-lock terms, which often come with lower fees.

Cons

- Your loan might be sold to another company after closing, but don't panic—your original terms are still legally binding.

How Does a FICO or Credit Score Affect Me When Buying a Home?

As we've touched on before, your credit score is one of the key factors lenders consider when you're applying for a big-ticket loan like a mortgage or auto loan. In most cases, the better your score, the better the interest rate you'll be offered, especially when it comes to buying property. But here's something people don't always realize: You could qualify for a lower rate and not be offered it, simply because you don't know what to ask for. I've seen this tactic firsthand. It's not always about what the *lender* knows—it's about what *you* don't know. That's one of the reasons I put this book together: to give you the tools to spot opportunities, ask the right questions, and secure a deal that truly reflects your financial standing and is fair. Of course, if you are paying for your home entirely in cash, this may not apply to you. But for most of us using a loan, keep in mind that different types of mortgages come with their own minimum credit score requirements, so it's always smart to know where you stand before you apply. Refer to figure 5.1 for information on each type of loan.

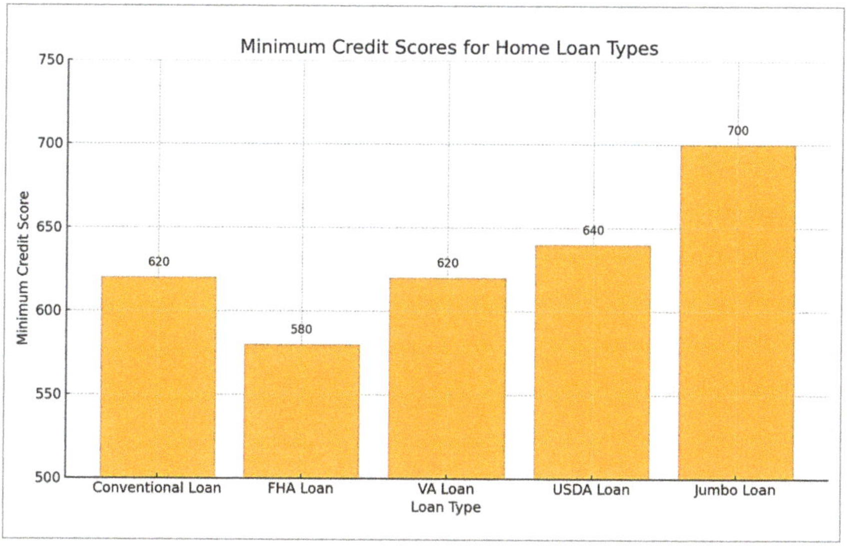

Figure 5.1 Source: Your Blueprint for Financial Literacy

Figure 5.1 compares the typical minimum credit scores lenders require for several common mortgage types. Figure 5.2 on the following page illustrates how credit scores can affect mortgage interest rates and the total interest paid over the life of a 30-year mortgage.

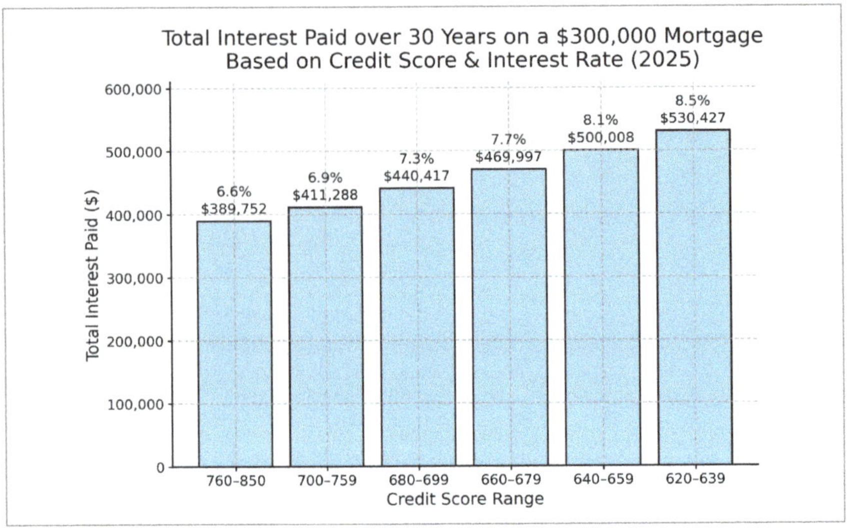

Figure 5.2 Source: Your Blueprint for Financial Literacy

Minimum Credit Scores for Different Home Loans

Understanding the type of home loan you're applying for—and what credit score is needed—is key to knowing where you stand. Here's a quick breakdown of common loan types and their typical credit score requirements:[75]

Conventional loans. These are standard loans not backed by the government and are offered by traditional banks and lenders. Many lenders will consider a score as low as 620, but you may need a stronger income or a larger down payment if you're on the lower end of the score range.

FHA loans. Backed by the Federal Housing Administration, these loans are a solid option for first-time buyers or those with lower credit. You could qualify with a score between 500 and 579 if you're putting 10% down, or with just 3.5% down if your score is 580 or above.

USDA loans. Offered through the US Department of Agriculture, these loans support low- to moderate-income buyers in eligible

75 Libby Well, "What Is a Good Credit Score to Buy a House?," Bankrate, June 26, 2025, https://www.bankrate.com/real-estate/what-credit-score-do-you-need-to-buy-a-house/.

rural areas. While 640 is the standard minimum score, some lenders may accept lower scores with extra financial documentation.

VA loans. Designed for veterans, active-duty service members, and their families, these loans are backed by the Department of Veterans Affairs. There's no official minimum credit score required by the VA, but most lenders set their minimum around 620.

Jumbo loans. If you are financing a home that exceeds standard lending limits (currently $766,550 in most areas), you'll need a strong credit score—usually 700 or higher—to qualify. Because of the larger loan size, lenders take on more risk and require higher scores.

Tips to Improve Your Credit Score[76]

1. Review your credit report for errors. Mistakes happen—check your report regularly and dispute any inaccuracies.
2. Pay down existing credit card balances. Lowering your credit utilization ratio can give your score a healthy boost.
3. Always pay your bills on time. Your payment history is one of the biggest factors in your credit score.
4. Keep old accounts open. Older accounts help build a longer credit history, which is good for your score.
5. Avoid opening new credit lines or applying for large loans. Hard inquiries and new debt can temporarily lower your score.

What's a Debt-to-Income Ratio?

Investopedia defines the **debt-to-income (DTI) ratio** as "the percentage of your gross monthly income that goes toward paying your monthly debt obligations."[77] Lenders use this number to

76 Well, "What Is a Good Credit Score to Buy a House?"

77 Lorraine Roberte, "Debt-to-Income (DTI) Ratio: What's Good and How To Calculate It," Investopedia, April 9, 2025, https://www.investopedia.com/terms/d/dti.asp.

measure your ability to manage monthly payments and repay borrowed money.

A lower DTI generally signals a healthy balance between income and debt, showing lenders that you're more likely to manage additional loans responsibly. A high DTI might indicate that you're stretched too thin financially, which could hurt your chances of qualifying for new credit. For example, if your DTI is 15%, that means 15% of your gross monthly income goes toward debt payments, like your mortgage, car loan, or credit card bills. The lower this percentage, the better your odds of getting approved for loans with good terms.

Most lenders prefer a DTI ratio of 36% or less, with no more than 28% going toward housing expenses. The highest DTI allowed to still qualify for a mortgage is generally around 43%, depending on the loan type and lender.[78]

One limitation of the DTI ratio is that it doesn't factor in the interest rates tied to each debt source. For instance, credit cards often have higher interest rates than student loans, but both are included equally in your DTI calculation. Reducing your interest payments, for example, by transferring balances to a lower-interest card—can lower your monthly payments and improve your DTI, even if your total outstanding debt stays the same.

Sophia's Monthly Financial Picture

Let's use an example of Sophia's DTI calculations.

- Total monthly debt payments: $2,400
- Gross monthly income: $8,500
- Mortgage payment: $1,800
- Credit card payment: $250
- Car loan payment: $350

78 Roberte, "Debt-to-Income (DTI) Ratio: What's Good and How To Calculate It."

This is the formula for the DTI ratio:

(Total monthly debt payments ÷ gross monthly income) × 100 = DTI

In Sophia's case, her DTI calculation would look like this:

($2,400 ÷ $8,500) × 100 = 28.24%

Sophia's DTI is 28.24%, which is within the preferred range for mortgage approval. Lenders would likely view her as a lower-risk borrower.

Remember, don't bite off more than you can chew. A manageable DTI ratio ensures you aren't overextending yourself and helps maintain financial stability.

How Do I Choose a Good Real Estate Agent? What's the Difference Between a Real Estate Broker, Real Estate Agent, and a Realtor?

According to Investopedia, a **real estate agent** is a licensed professional who facilitates property transactions, represents clients in negotiations, and helps connect buyers with sellers.[79] Agents typically earn a commission based on the property's sale price, so their income depends on the volume and value of transactions they close. In most states, agents must work under a **licensed broker**, someone who has more training and experience.[80] Real estate agents often specialize in residential or commercial properties, and their responsibilities vary depending on whether they represent the buyer or the seller. Listing agents (representing the seller) assist with pricing, staging, and marketing properties, while buyer's agents help clients find homes within their budget and make realistic offers.

79 Troy Segal, "The Differences Between a Real Estate Agent, a Broker, and a Realtor," Investopedia, July 1, 2025, https://www.investopedia.com/ask/answers/101314/what-are-differences-among-real-estate-agent-broker-and-realtor.asp.

80 Segal, "The Differences Between a Real Estate Agent, a Broker, and a Realtor."

Both agents manage communication between parties, help with inspections, and guide the process to closing. It's important to know who the agent represents in a deal—buyer, seller, or both. Some states allow dual agency, but others have banned it due to potential conflicts of interest. Agents are required to disclose who they represent. For reference, dual agency is illegal in eight states: Alaska, Colorado, Florida, Kansas, Maryland, Texas, Vermont, and Wyoming.[81] Choosing a trustworthy agent is critical. Unfortunately, not all agents act in their clients' best interests. I had an agent work behind my back with a seller to increase their commission. I reported the agent and backed out of the deal. Thankfully, I've also worked with excellent agents like Elizabeth Monteleone of Monument Sotheby's International Realty. Don't skip your due diligence; walk through the property thoroughly, ask questions, and always get a home inspection.

Common Red Flags with Real Estate Agents

- Beware of inflated property values. Some agents overprice homes to win listings. Check comps in the area or hire an appraiser to confirm the home's market value. Online platforms like Zillow or Trulia can provide a good starting point.
- Look out for fake buyers. Agents may claim they have a perfect buyer lined up. Ask direct questions to confirm. If the agent seems evasive, take that as a red flag.
- Be wary of misleading listings. Agents sometimes exaggerate or make claims about properties they haven't personally seen. Watch for terms like *BATVAI* (buyer's agent to verify all information) or *IDRBNG* (information deemed reliable but not guaranteed), which shift the burden of verification to the buyer.

81 Segal, "The Differences Between a Real Estate Agent, a Broker, and a Realtor."

Real Estate Agents Versus Real Estate Brokers

The difference between agents and brokers varies by state. In general, an **agent** is someone who has completed basic training and passed a real estate exam. A **broker** has additional education, including passing a broker's exam, and often has more experience. Brokers can operate independently and supervise other agents, whereas agents typically work under brokers. In some states, like Colorado and New Mexico, all real estate professionals must be licensed as brokers.[82]

Real Estate Agents Versus Realtors

A **Realtor** is a member of the National Association of Realtors. Realtors must follow the association's code of ethics and are often considered more accountable due to this affiliation. While all Realtors are agents or brokers, not all agents or brokers are Realtors. Members of a local or state board are also required to carry the Realtor title.[83]

Understanding these roles helps you know who you're working with and what to expect throughout your real estate journey.

How Much Does a Real Estate Agent Cost?

This isn't usually the first question buyers ask—but it should be. NerdWallet explains it well: Real estate commissions are typically split between the listing agent, the buyer's agent, and their respective brokerages. If the commission is 6%, it might be broken down like this[84]:

- 1.5% to the listing agent
- 1.5% to the listing broker

82 Segal, "The Differences Between a Real Estate Agent, a Broker, and a Realtor."

83 Segal, "The Differences Between a Real Estate Agent, a Broker, and a Realtor."

84 Holden Lewis, "Real Estate Agent Commission: How Your Agent Gets Paid," NerdWallet, updated August 17, 2024, https://www.nerdwallet.com/article/mortgages/real-estate-agent-commission.

- 1.5% to the buyer's agent
- 1.5% to the buyer's broker

These percentages can vary depending on the agreement. As mentioned earlier, brokers are licensed agents who've taken additional courses and passed a separate exam, allowing them to run their own firms or supervise other agents.

Traditionally, sellers have paid the commission for both the buyer's and seller's agents as part of the closing costs. While buyers don't directly pay their agent, that commission cost can still affect them. Sellers often build it into the price of the home. Recently, this practice has come under legal scrutiny. Class action lawsuits argued that NAR's commission system inflated costs and limited sellers' ability to negotiate. In March 2024, a class action settlement was reached, with NAR agreeing to pay $418 million and eliminate long-standing MLS commission rules. Among the changes, buyer agents must now sign written agreements before showing properties, and compensation offers are no longer displayed on Multiple Listing Service (MLS) systems.[85] Whether you're buying or selling, it's smart to understand how agent commissions work so you can ask the right questions and avoid paying fees you shouldn't be responsible for.

Do I Really Need a Real Estate Agent?

While it's not usually the first question that comes to mind, it is one every first-time buyer should ask early in the process. If you're new to the home-buying process, my advice is simple: *Don't try to go it alone.* Buying a home without an agent can be risky, especially when you're not familiar with all the moving parts. A trained, licensed real estate agent—specifically a **buyer's agent**—works for

85 Alex Veiga, "Real Estate Lawsuit Settlement Upends Decadeslong Policies That Helped Set Agent Commissions," AP News, March 15, 2024, https://apnews.com/article/national-association-of-realtors-agent-commissions-lawsuits-d62a66cb80639be3c4c3b429053a22c5.

you. Their job is to protect your interests, help you avoid mistakes, and guide you through what could be the biggest purchase of your life. According to Bankrate, here are just a few things a buyer's agent can do that you'd otherwise have to tackle on your own:[86]

- Agents help find the right home within your budget and needs. Sure, real estate websites are helpful, but agents dig deeper. They can tell you whether the price is fair based on comparable homes nearby—and that alone can save you thousands.
- They uncover important neighborhood details. This includes things a seller might not be up-front about. An experienced agent knows how to spot red flags and steer you away from problems.
- Your agent negotiates your offer and makes sure you're not overpaying. They'll also help write in key protections (called contingencies) that safeguard you as a buyer.
- They guide you through the inspection. Your agent can help you ask for the right repairs or credits if something turns up.
- They review all the paperwork. Real estate documents are often full of legal terms and fine print that can be overwhelming if you're unfamiliar with them.
- Agents request disclosures that the seller may be legally required to provide. A new buyer may not even know to ask for these.

Let me be blunt: Home buying is a high-stakes process. Mistakes can cost you time, stress, and serious money. Having someone experienced in your corner isn't just helpful; it's smart. I once ran

86 Sarah Li Cain, "Do I Need a Real Estate Agent to Buy a House?," Bankrate, January 11, 2025, https://www.bankrate.com/real-estate/should-i-buy-house-without-realtor/.

into a seller who was secretly acting as both the agent and the owner—without disclosing it. Thankfully, my broker caught it and handled it legally. But it goes to show, there are sharks in these waters, and a good agent is your lifeguard.

What's a Home Inspection, and Do I Need One?

Yes and yes! A home inspection is one of the smartest steps you can take, especially as a first-time buyer. According to Investopedia, a home inspection contingency gives buyers the right to hire a licensed inspector who checks for serious and minor issues before the sale is final.[87] This isn't just a "nice to have"—it's a safeguard. Home inspections can uncover dangerous issues like faulty wiring or mold, which could pose serious health or safety risks.

Most contracts give you around seven days after the inspection to walk away from the deal without penalty if major problems are found. Inspectors usually check everything from the roof to the foundation, including the plumbing, electrical, HVAC, and structural components. That's why this clause is often built into purchase contracts—it gives buyers the ability to back out if the home has hidden issues. From personal experience, I've found that inspectors certified to conduct FHA inspections tend to be especially thorough. And when it comes to newly built homes, there are typically multiple inspection stages:[88]

- Foundation—before the concrete is poured, allowing for checks on the foundation's preparation and structural components
- Framing—before insulation and drywall are installed, allowing for checks on the structure and mechanical system

87 Amy Fontinelle, "What Is a Home Inspection Contingency and Why Is It Important?," Investopedia, June 30, 2024, https://www.investopedia.com/articles/mortgages-real-estate/08/home-inspection.asp.

88 Fontinelle, "What Is a Home Inspection Contingency and Why Is It Important?"

- Final walk-through—before the closing, when the home is nearing completion, allowing for a complete inspection of the finished home

A home inspection doesn't just protect your money—it protects your peace of mind.

What's Included in a Home Inspection?

Not all inspectors are created equal. A good one should check key systems, note any issues, and give you a clear report. Inspections typically take two to three hours, and *you should always be present.* You'll learn more by seeing issues firsthand and can ask questions on the spot.

I once sold a property where the buyer's inspector found safety hazards that had to be corrected because it was an FHA loan. If I hadn't fixed them, the deal would've fallen through, and that report would've haunted the property for years. Lesson learned—cutting corners costs more in the long run.

A solid inspection report will highlight several areas:[89]

- Major versus minor issues
- Safety hazards
- Items to monitor
- Maintenance tips for first-time buyers

What Does a Home Inspector Look For?

Here are the most common areas covered in home inspection reports:[90]

89 Fontinelle, "What Is a Home Inspection Contingency and Why Is It Important?"
90 Fontinelle, "What Is a Home Inspection Contingency and Why Is It Important?"

Exterior

- Walls and siding—look for cracks, missing panels, or soil too close to the home.
- Foundation—check indirectly for cracks or uneven settling.
- Grading—ensure water slopes away from the house.
- Garage—test doors, ventilation, and any installed appliances (like water heaters).
- Roof—inspect for missing shingles, poor sealing, and gutter issues.

Tip—always hire a licensed roofer for repairs. You'll likely get a longer warranty and better work. My property manager had both a contractor and a licensed roofer provide quotes for repairing a roof. The contractor offered a one-year warranty, while the licensed roofer offered a ten-year warranty. You can probably guess which option we chose.

Interior

- Plumbing—test water pressure, inspect visible pipes, and note potential future issues.
- Electrical—check outlets and panels and make sure safety features like ground fault circuit interrupters are installed.
- HVAC—estimate the age and condition of systems and check for insulation and asbestos.
- Water heater—verify secure installation and condition.
- Laundry—ensure proper dryer ventilation to reduce fire risk.

- Fire safety—check garage walls, smoke detectors, and fire-rated materials.
- Bathrooms—look for leaks, proper ventilation, and mold risks.

Pro tip—some kitchen appliances may be tested as part of a home inspection. Always ask what's included.

What's Not Included in a Standard Inspection?

Inspectors don't usually open walls or dig into sewer lines. They also don't test for mold, asbestos, lead, radon, or termites, so you'll need a separate pest inspection. If an inspector spots red flags, they'll recommend calling a specialist.[91]

Your Options After the Inspection

Once you receive the report, you have three options:

Walk away. If the issues are deal-breakers, and your contract includes an inspection contingency, you don't have to move forward with the purchase.

Negotiate. Ask the seller to fix the problems, lower the price, or give you a credit at closing.

Plan repairs. This is especially applicable if the home is sold as-is or if the bank owns it.

Important—you're not legally required to fix issues, but major defects—electrical, structural, or pest-related—could stop your loan from going through.

How Do I Find a Home Inspector?

Tobie Stanger of Consumer Reports makes a great point: Don't wait until you have an accepted offer to start looking for a home

91 Fontinelle, "What Is a Home Inspection Contingency and Why Is It Important?"

inspector. Interview a few in advance—you want someone experienced and detail oriented who will work in your best interest.[92]

Watch out for agent referrals. Real estate agents might suggest inspectors, but that can be a conflict of interest. If your agent is more focused on closing the deal than uncovering problems, you could get shortchanged. Unless you truly trust your agent, it's smart to do your own research.

Find a great home inspector. Ask friends who recently bought a home. Also, check sites like Yelp, Angi, or Nextdoor for reviews. You can also look for certified professionals through national organizations like these:

- ASHI, American Society of Home Inspectors
- InterNACHI, International Association of Certified Home Inspectors
- Consumers' Checkbook, available in select cities

Pro tip—search the inspector's name along with words like *complaints* or *reviews.*

Remember that credentials are great but not everything. Certifications like those from ASHI or InterNACHI mean an inspector passed exams and completed real inspections, but a certification doesn't guarantee thoroughness. Consumer Reports once hired twelve certified inspectors for the same home with twenty-eight known issues—none of the inspectors found them all. Knowledge matters, but attention to detail is everything.

92 Tobie Stanger, "How to Choose a Home Inspector," Consumer Reports, updated May 8, 2025, https://www.consumerreports.org/home-inspections/how-to-choose-a-home-inspector-a7413938402.

Compare sample reports. Ask to see a sample report. The best inspectors go beyond basic checklists and explain what they found clearly and thoroughly. If the sample report is vague or filled with general tips like "seal your windows," keep looking.

Check for experience and extras. More years in the field usually means a better eye for issues. If you're buying an older home, you might want an inspector with a background in construction or engineering. Expect to pay between $300 and $1,000, depending on the home and the inspector's services. Some use drones or infrared cameras; ask whether those are included or cost extra. Specialized tests for mold, radon, or pests may require additional inspectors and fees.[93]

What's the Closing Cost, and What's Included?

Once you're at the closing stage, you're just steps away from homeownership—but there's one more hurdle: **closing costs**. These are the extra expenses (beyond the home's price) that buyers and sellers pay to finalize a real estate deal. According to Investopedia, closing costs may include fees like the loan origination charge, title insurance, appraisal, taxes, credit reports, and more. Legally, your lender must give you a **disclosure** at least three business days before settlement.[94] This document outlines all the fees so there are no surprises.

93 Stanger, "How to Choose a Home Inspector."

94 Investopedia Team, "Closing Costs: What They Are and How Much They Cost," Investopedia, October 7, 2024, https://www.investopedia.com/terms/c/closingcosts.asp.

How Much Will You Pay in Closing Costs?

Closing costs typically range from 3% to 6% of the home's purchase price. For example, on a $300,000 home, that could mean $9,000 to $18,000 in additional expenses. While buyers usually cover most of these costs, you can negotiate with the seller to contribute, especially in a buyer's market. Some buyers even roll the costs into their mortgage. And if you're a first-time homebuyer, you may qualify for state-level assistance programs to help reduce up-front expenses.

Closing costs can add up quickly, so it helps to know exactly what you're paying for. Here are some of the most common fees you might see at the closing table and what each one covers.[95]

Common Closing Costs

Depending on the loan type, you might also see these fees:

- Loan origination fees are administrative costs to set up your mortgage.
- Title insurance and title searches protect against future ownership disputes.
- Appraisal fees cover the assessment of the home's market value.
- Credit report fees are associated with the lender checking your credit with major bureaus.
- Recording fees are paid to the local government to update public records.
- Escrow deposits usually cover two months of taxes and insurance up front.
- Homeowners' insurance is typically required to be prepaid at closing.

95 Investopedia Team, "Closing Costs: What They Are and How Much They Cost."

- Private mortgage insurance may be required if your down payment is under 20%.
- Underwriting fees cover the lender's reviews of your financials for final approval.
- Transfer taxes are charged to legally transfer property ownership.
- Prepaid interest covers any interest before your first mortgage payment.
- FHA mortgage insurance is insurance required for FHA loans that protects the lender if you default.
- VA funding fee is a one-time fee paid by most VA loan borrowers to help keep the program running.
- Homeowners' association transfer fees charge for transferring HOA ownership records to the new owner.

How to Save on Closing Costs

Buyers aren't stuck paying the full sticker price. Here are a few ways to cut costs:[96]

- Shop around. Get quotes from different lenders, insurers, and title companies.
- Schedule wisely. Closing at the end of the month lowers prepaid interest.
- Negotiate with the seller. This is especially helpful if the property's been on the market for a while.
- Question junk fees. Ask your lender to explain or waive any questionable charges like processing or document-handling fees.

96 Investopedia Team, "Closing Costs: What They Are and How Much They Cost."

Buying a home is a big financial commitment—understanding and managing your closing costs can help you save thousands and start your homeownership journey on the right foot. Refer to figure 5.3 for an example of a closing document.

Personal Finance Closing Cost Example

Buyer Closing Costs

Cost Item	Amount ($)
Loan Origination Fee (1%)	$3,000.00
Appraisal Fee	$500.00
Credit Report Fee	$50.00
Title Insurance	$1,000.00
Escrow Deposit (2 Months)	$800.00
Homeowner's Insurance (1st Year)	$1,200.00
Prepaid Interest	$300.00
Recording Fees	$250.00
Survey Fee	$400.00
Underwriting Fee	$600.00
Pest Inspection	$150.00
Home Inspection	$500.00
Attorney Fee	$1,000.00
Total Buyer Closing Costs	$9,750.00
Net Buyer Closing Cost After $3,000 Credit	$6,750.00

Seller Proceeds Summary

Item	Amount ($)
Home Sale Price	$300,000.00
Outstanding Mortgage	$-50,000.00
Closing Credit to Buyer	$-3,000.00
Estimated Seller Closing Costs (6% agent fees)	$-18,000.00
Net Seller Proceeds	$229,000.00

Figure 5.3 Source: Your Blueprint for Financial Literacy

After the Closing Cost Is Paid, Do I Own the House?

According to Compass Mortgage, when you buy a home using a mortgage, you are indeed the legal homeowner.[97] You can make decisions about decor, remodeling, landscaping, and more. However,

97 Compass Mortgage, "First-Time Homebuyer FAQ: If I Have a Mortgage, Do I Own My Home?," Compass Mortgage (blog), August 31, 2023, https://www.compmort.com/first-time-homebuyer-faq-if-i-have-a-mortgage-do-i-own-my-home/.

the lender still holds a financial interest in the property until the loan is fully paid.

At closing, you will sign a few key documents that outline your rights—and your lender's—regarding the home. The **mortgage note** is your official promise to repay the loan. It includes the loan amount, repayment terms, and potential penalties if you fail to uphold your end of the agreement. Your **deed of trust** lays out both your responsibilities and the lender's, including the lender's right to foreclose if you default. While the lender uses your home as collateral, you remain the rightful owner—provided you stay current with your mortgage payments.

So, yes, you own the home, but until it is paid off, the bank still has a stake in it.

CHAPTER 5 KEY BENEFITS

You should now have a better understanding of the following:

- ✓ **Step-by-step guidance.** Knowledge of the home-buying process, from down payments to closing costs, enables you to approach real estate transactions confidently.
- ✓ **Financial preparedness.** Insights into mortgages, credit scores, and cosigners will prepare you for the financial responsibilities of homeownership.
- ✓ **Agent insights.** Understanding the roles of real estate agents and inspectors will help you navigate the home-buying process with confidence.
- ✓ **Ownership clarity.** You know what closing costs entail and what it truly means to own a home after the purchase.

Source: Your Blueprint for Financial Literacy

Chapter 6

How Do I Buy a Car?

So, you're thinking about buying a car? Buckle up—because the road to car ownership isn't always smooth. It can be exciting but also a bit overwhelming if you don't know what to look for. Let me take you back to my first car-buying experience. Picture this: college days, limited funds, and zero car-buying knowledge. My friend James Jackson Jr.—a.k.a. "Cheetah" (don't ask me why they called him Cheetah; I still don't know)—took me to a local car auction. We walked in with $1,500 and drove out with an Oldsmobile Cutlass Ciera.

Believe me, that car put the "old" in Oldsmobile. It lasted about two years before the engine decided it'd had enough of me. That first ride taught me a lot, and since then, I've bought cars in various cities—from New York City to London and beyond. One thing I've learned is that whether you're in a city with solid public transportation or in a place where buses come once a day (if you're lucky), owning a car can be either a luxury or a necessity.

Q&A SESSION

Do I Need a Car?

After reading the title of this chapter, you might think you've already answered the question. But let's take a moment to look at the pros and cons before jumping to a conclusion. According to How to Money, there are some solid arguments both for and against living without a car.[98]

Advantages of Living Without a Car

- You save money. Between insurance, gas, maintenance, and taxes, owning a car eats up a big chunk of your budget. It's often the second biggest expense after housing. Going car-free could free up funds for saving, investing, or just breathing a little easier.
- Life gets simpler. Cars come with drama—unexpected repairs, oil changes, inspections, parking struggles, and more. Drop the car, and you drop the hassle. Even ditching one vehicle in a multicar household can reduce stress.
- Your health may improve. Leaving or not using the car could mean more walking or biking. That's free exercise and mental clarity. Less time behind the wheel means less stress from traffic. It's good for the body and mind.
- It's better for the planet. Transportation accounts for over a quarter of greenhouse gas emissions in the US. Even replacing short trips—many under three miles—with walking or biking helps the environment.
- You may connect more with your community. Walking and biking give you the chance to notice your surroundings, chat with neighbors, and discover local gems you'd never see from behind the wheel.
- Say goodbye to traffic. The average driver spends nearly one hundred hours a year in traffic. That's time you'll never get back. Skip the car—and the traffic headache.

98 Britney DiTocco, "The Pros and Cons of Living Without a Car," How to Money, February 4, 2025, https://www.howtomoney.com/no-car-no-problem/.

Disadvantages of Living Without a Car

- Mass transit is not available in some areas. If you're in a rural town or a suburb with little public transit, living car-free can be tough. If your job is far away, you may even consider moving closer to save on gas and time.
- You'll deal with the elements. Walking or biking means exposure to rain, snow, heat—whatever the sky throws your way. Having an extra outfit or checking the weather daily helps, but it's still a change from the climate-controlled bubble of a car.
- You'll need to plan more. Spontaneous trips become trickier. Public transit routes need to be studied. Carpools must be arranged. Apps like Uber and Lyft help, but planning still takes extra effort.

It might just be the freedom you didn't know you needed. Still not sure? Keep reading—the next section dives into what you should know if you do decide to buy a car.

What's the Best Place to Start When Looking for a Car to Purchase?

According to Investopedia, buying a car has some perks over leasing—but if it's your first rodeo, you might not know what's coming. There's more to it than picking a shiny vehicle and driving off into the sunset. There are different ways to buy and pay for a car, and yes—plenty of paperwork to make it legal.

Here's what you need to do *before* the test-drives and price haggling begin:[99]

99 Michelle L. Black, "Heading to the Car Dealership? Get a Great Deal by Following These 9 Steps," Investopedia, February 18, 2025, https://www.investopedia.com/how-to-buy-a-car-from-a-dealership-8687310.

- Set a realistic budget.
- Decide if you're paying cash or getting a loan.
- Figure out your down payment.
- Know the type of car you're looking for.
- Choose where to shop: a dealer or private seller.
- Understand what can be negotiated (spoiler—not everything).
- Know what happens after the sale, like registration and insurance.

Now, if you're planning to finance your ride, it's time to check that credit score again (hello, FICO, my old friend). Better credit equals better loan rates. Sound familiar? That's because it's true in almost every major financial decision you'll make.

Buying a New Car from a Dealership

Let me tell you—buying a new car from a dealership is not for the impatient. It can take a while, but this does come with some real perks. At a dealership, you can test-drive a bunch of cars, compare financing deals, and maybe even snag a manufacturer incentive or discount.

Even if you have *no credit*, you can still buy a car—but be ready for a higher interest rate and a bigger down payment. If your credit needs some love, consider waiting or adding a cosigner. Just make sure that person knows they're sharing your financial baggage.

Pro tip—check out your own bank for financing options. I financed my car through my bank and walked out with a better deal than what the dealership was offering. Loyalty sometimes pays off.

At a dealership, you can test-drive a bunch of cars, compare financing deals, and maybe even snag a manufacturer incentive or discount. Buying online from a dealership is growing in popularity too. Some dealers even deliver the car for a test-drive—but heads up: That delivery may come with fees.

Calculate your budget. A car isn't only the sticker price. You've also got to budget for these items:[100]

- Monthly loan payments
- Auto insurance
- Property taxes (in some states)
- Fuel, maintenance, and repairs
- Registration and inspection fees

Some of these costs can be rolled into your loan, but things like taxes and certain fees might need to come out of your pocket.

Check your credit. Your credit score will play a huge role in the loan offers you get. Once again, a better score means lower interest rates and more flexible terms. If your credit's looking rough, consider working on it before applying—or prepare for a bigger financial burden.[101]

Choose the vehicle and features you want. Make a list before you step on the lot. Know what type of vehicle you want, how many people you need to haul around, what features matter to you (fuel economy, cargo space, sunroof, etc.), and whether you've got a driveway or street parking. The more prepared you are, the less likely you'll be swayed into something you don't need or, worse, can't afford.[102]

---

100 Black, "Heading to the Car Dealership? Get a Great Deal by Following These 9 Steps."

101 Black, "Heading to the Car Dealership? Get a Great Deal by Following These 9 Steps."

102 Black, "Heading to the Car Dealership? Get a Great Deal by Following These 9 Steps."

Buying a Car Online

Back in the day, buying a car meant showing up at a lot and kicking tires until your toes were sore. Now? You can shop for cars in your pajamas. Here are some online spots where you can find both new and used cars:[103]

- Facebook Marketplace
- local Facebook deal groups
- Craigslist
- auto trader websites
- car-buying concierge services
- official dealership websites

If you're hunting for a used car, those community and classified-style sites might be your best bet. For new cars, it's often best to go directly through a dealership or concierge service. Just remember that even with online car buying, you'll still need to leave your house at some point—maybe to test-drive the car, get it inspected by a mechanic, or sign paperwork.

> Pro tip—always get a car inspected before finalizing a deal, especially if it's a private sale. Some things can't be seen in a photo (like that weird smell under the back seat).

Buying a Used Car with Cash

If you can buy a car with cash—congratulations, you're doing something right! Paying cash means no monthly payment, no interest, and no lenders involved in your business.

103 Jessica Ullrich, "How to Buy a Car Online," Investopedia, December 30, 2024, https://www.investopedia.com/how-to-buy-a-car-online-7974497.

Here's what to consider:[104]

- Know how much you can actually spend (not your "wishful thinking" budget).
- Have your money ready—whether it's in savings, a tax refund, or the proceeds from selling your sneaker collection.
- Use a cashier's check or certified check if possible. It's safer than carrying actual cash, and it gives you a paper trail.
- If you're meeting a private seller, *meet in a public place*—a well-lit parking lot or even a police station is ideal.[105]

Fun fact—dealers love when you show up with cash; just don't tell them that too early. Let them talk numbers first, then pull out the ace card.

Refer to figure 6.1 for a comparison of the key differences between buying a car online and purchasing from a dealership, highlighting what to expect in terms of convenience, pricing, flexibility, and risk.

104 Lisa Smith, "Should I Buy a New or Used Car?," Investopedia, January 6, 2024, https://www.investopedia.com/articles/pf/07/neworusedcar.asp.

105 Shannon Bradley, "How To Buy a Used Car From a Private Seller," NerdWallet, updated November 12, 2025, https://www.nerdwallet.com/article/loans/auto-loans/tips-for-buying-a-used-car-from-a-private-seller.

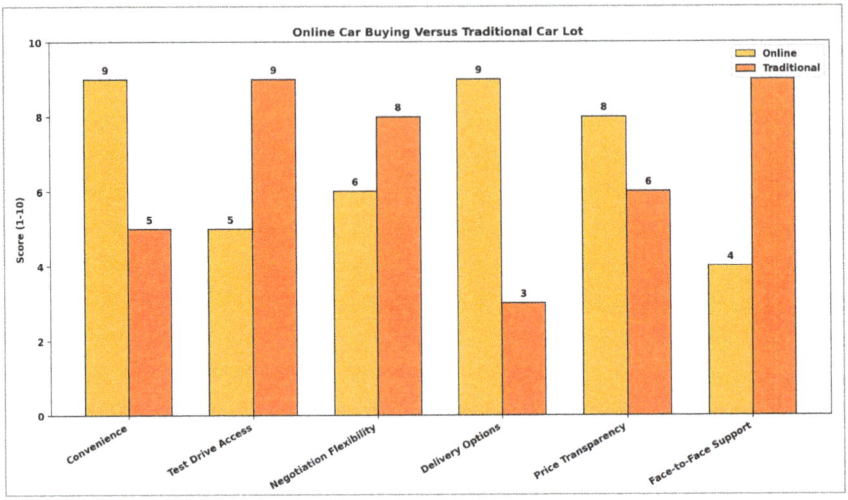

Figure 6.1 Source: Your Blueprint for Financial Literacy

Buying a Car with a Credit Card

You might be thinking, "Can I just swipe my way into a new ride?" The short answer is...maybe. It all depends on your credit limit, your card issuer's policy, and the dealership's willingness to accept plastic for such a large transaction. Some buyers are able to charge the down payment—or even the full price of the car—if their credit limit is high enough. Sounds great, right? You might even earn points, cash back, or airline miles—imagine getting a free flight just for buying your car! For example, if your card gives 1% cash back, a $10,000 charge would net you $100 in rewards.

But before you swipe your credit card, keep in mind the interest. Car loans usually come with lower interest rates than credit cards, especially if you've got decent credit. So unless your card has a 0% introductory offer or you're planning to pay off the balance quickly, the rewards might be wiped out by high interest or annual fees.

Pro tip—if you're considering this route, call your credit

card company first. Make sure they'll allow the charge and ask what rate you'll be charged. You don't want a surprise bill that hits harder than your car insurance premium.[106]

Buying a Car Out of State

Sometimes the car you want isn't out of budget—it's out of state. And that's totally legal. But just because this is legal doesn't mean it's hassle-free. If you buy a car across state lines, be prepared for extra steps. First, you'll pay sales tax to the state where you register the car, not where you bought it. You'll also need to handle the registration, license plates, inspection (if your state requires it), and proof of insurance once the car makes it home. Getting the car delivered or picking it up yourself is also part of the equation. Depending on the distance, you'll either need to book a transport service or make a mini road trip out of it. Remember that the Department of Motor Vehicles (DMV) doesn't care how far you traveled—the paperwork still needs to be done right.[107]

If you don't register, inspect, or insure your vehicle properly, you could end up with tickets or fines before your new ride even hits the road.

Buying a Used Car from a Dealer

Shopping for a used car from a dealer? Good choice—if you know what to look for. You still need to check your budget, know how much you can put down, and compare financing offers. Watch out for "buy here, pay here" deals. They sound convenient, but the interest rates are often sky high. If your credit's not great, you might still get approved, but it'll likely cost more long term. Always

106 Ted Rossman, "Can I Buy a Car with a Credit Card?," Bankrate, February 5, 2025, https://www.bankrate.com/credit-cards/advice/buy-car-with-credit-card/.

107 Progressive Insurance, "Buying a Car Out of State," Progressive Answers, accessed August 25, 2025, https://www.progressive.com/answers/buying-a-car-out-of-state/.

inspect the car thoroughly. Test-drive it. Ask for a Carfax report. If anything feels shady, walk away. And don't forget that even used cars can come with warranties—but make sure you read the fine print so you know what's actually covered.

> A used-car warranty might sound great—until you realize it covers about as much as a five-dollar umbrella in a thunderstorm. Read carefully.

How to Evaluate and Buy Potential Cars

Test-drive and inspect the car. This is your moment, so don't skip it. A test-drive helps you feel how the car runs and whether you can see yourself in it long term.

Use this time wisely:

- Confirm that the features you want are actually there.
- Check for interior and exterior damage.
- See how the car handles at different speeds.
- Make sure you're comfortable behind the wheel.[108]

> Always ask for the vehicle history report. It tells you more than the salesperson ever will. The report should list accidents, repairs, and whether the car's been treated like royalty or rode hard and put away wet.

Negotiate with salespeople. Here's where it gets tricky. That friendly salesperson, their job is to sell you everything—and then some. The more you spend, the better their commission. You've

108 Keith Barry, "How to Test-Drive a New or Used Car," Consumer Reports, April 7, 2025, https://www.consumerreports.org/cars/buying-a-car/how-to-test-drive-a-new-or-used-car-a4558551981.

got to come prepared, not only with money but with a game plan. Use these key tips to keep you in control:

- Stick to your budget. Don't let slick talk stretch your wallet.
- Know your numbers. Research average prices for the vehicle you want before stepping onto the lot.
- Shop around. Get quotes from several dealerships, then use them to your advantage.
- Be ready to walk away. If the deal isn't right, keep it moving.
- Look at the total price. Consider more than just the monthly payment. Some deals look great until you see the fine print.

Remember, rushing into a deal is like rushing into a marriage—costly and hard to undo.

Watch for add-ons. After you negotiate the price, brace yourself. The finance person will likely pitch you extra products, like extended warranties or guaranteed asset protection (GAP) insurance. These add-ons sound good but can be major moneymakers for the dealership. Many of these add-ons you probably don't need. You might be better off putting that money into your emergency fund instead. If your car ever needs a repair, you'll have the cash ready. And if it doesn't? You've just grown your savings.

Parking your emergency fund in a high-yield savings account? Even better. That money won't just sit there—it'll work for you.

Finalize the deal. Once you've haggled and landed on a fair deal, don't rush to sign on the dotted line. Read everything—yes, everything. Contracts, loan terms, trade-in details—double-check them all. If you're trading in your old car, make sure the dealership honors the agreed value. Better yet, do your homework ahead of time to know what your car is worth. A dealership once offered me $2,300 for a trade-in. I donated the car to National Public Radio instead; they auctioned it for $5,600, and I got the full amount as a tax write-off. That's what I call a win-win.

Before you head to the dealership, pack smart. Take these items with you:

- Government-issued ID
- Proof of insurance
- Loan preapproval letter (if you have one)

Register your new or used vehicle. Some dealers will register your new or used car for you, giving you temporary tags so you can hit the road the same day. Others will hand you the paperwork and send you straight to DMV. Make sure you know what's expected before you drive off the lot. If you're buying from a private seller, registration, taxes, insurance, and all the DMV fun fall on you. Budget for the headache—and the fees.

Take ownership of your car. Sometimes you can drive off the lot the same day. Other times, you'll wait for delivery. Either way, inspect your new ride carefully, especially if it's delivered later. Look for scratches, dents, or anything that wasn't there before. You should also get a quick tour of the car's tech and features—yes, even how to sync your phone to Bluetooth. Many dealerships take care of the registration and plates for you, but depending on your state, they might need you to pay property tax first. Bottom line—ask questions, read the fine print, and don't leave until you know exactly what you're driving away with—literally and legally.[109]

Should I Buy a New or Used Car?

According to Investopedia, deciding whether to buy a new or used vehicle depends on several factors, including cost, financing terms, interest rates, depreciation, insurance, and long-term reliability. Let's take a closer look at the advantages and disadvantages of each to help you make an informed decision.[110]

Advantages of Buying a New Car

- Reliability and warranty. Most new cars include manufacturer warranties, giving you peace of mind if issues arise early in ownership.
- Roadside assistance. Many manufacturers offer free roadside assistance with new purchases.
- Updated features. New cars typically offer the latest technology, safety innovations, and fuel-efficiency standards.
- Financing incentives. Buyers with strong credit may qualify for low- or even zero-interest financing options through the manufacturer or dealer.

Disadvantages of Buying a New Car

- Higher up-front cost. New cars have a premium price, which translates to higher monthly loan payments and total interest over time.
- Depreciation. Depreciation is what happens when something loses value over time—kind of like how a

109 Consumer Reports, "How to Buy a Used Car Safely," Consumer Reports, March 19, 2025, https://www.consumerreports.org/cars/used-cars/buying-guide/.

110 Smith, "Should I Buy a New or Used Car?"

brand-new phone feels exciting on day one, but a year later, it's slower, has scratches, and isn't worth as much if you tried to sell it. Cars, electronics, and even houses can depreciate, depending on use, age, and condition. A new car can lose up to 10% of its value the moment it leaves the dealership and continues to depreciate rapidly.

- Insurance costs. Higher replacement values often result in increased insurance premiums.
- Loss of newness. Cosmetic wear and tear accumulates quickly. Meanwhile, your financial commitment remains.

Advantages of Buying a Used Car

- Lower purchase price. Most depreciation has already occurred, offering better value for money.
- Certified preowned options. Many certified used vehicles come with extended warranties and inspection guarantees.
- Reduced insurance costs. Lower vehicle value typically leads to lower premiums.

Disadvantages of Buying a Used Car

- Higher mileage. More mileage increases the likelihood of repairs and may shorten the car's remaining lifespan.
- Fewer options. It may be harder to find the exact combination of features and specifications you're looking for.
- Limited consumer protection. Depending on the age and condition of the vehicle, lemon laws, and return protections may not apply. Lemon laws are state rules that protect buyers who end up with a defective vehicle. If a new (and in some states, used) car has serious problems

that keep it from working as it should—and the manufacturer or dealer can't fix those problems after a reasonable number of tries—the law can require them to replace the car or give you your money back.

Additional Costs to Consider for New or Used Cars

- Unexpected repairs
- Fuel expenses
- Down payment
- Taxes, title, and registration fees
- Insurance premiums
- Scheduled maintenance
- Loan interest (if financing)

Maintenance and financing considerations. New vehicles typically require fewer repairs in the early years, but the initial cost—and often the interest—will be higher. Used vehicles may come with increased maintenance needs, but the lower purchase price and insurance premiums may offset those costs.

Why interest rates matter. Interest rates play a key role in total cost of ownership. While new-car loans generally offer lower rates, the higher vehicle price may still result in more total interest paid. Conversely, used-car loans may carry higher rates, but the smaller loan size may lead to lower overall costs.

Questions to Ask When Buying Used

- What is the current mileage?
- Has the car been in any accidents?

- Is it certified preowned?
- Are any aftermarket parts included?
- What kind of warranty is provided?
- What additional fees should I expect?

Take your time and do your research. Evaluate both the up-front and long-term financial impacts of buying new versus used. The right vehicle should meet your needs, offer reliability, and align with your budget.

Refer to figure 6.2 for a visual comparison of the estimated total cost of ownership between a new and a used vehicle over a five-year period. This includes depreciation, loan interest, maintenance, and insurance. These figures are estimates and can vary based on vehicle make, model, financing terms, and geographic location.

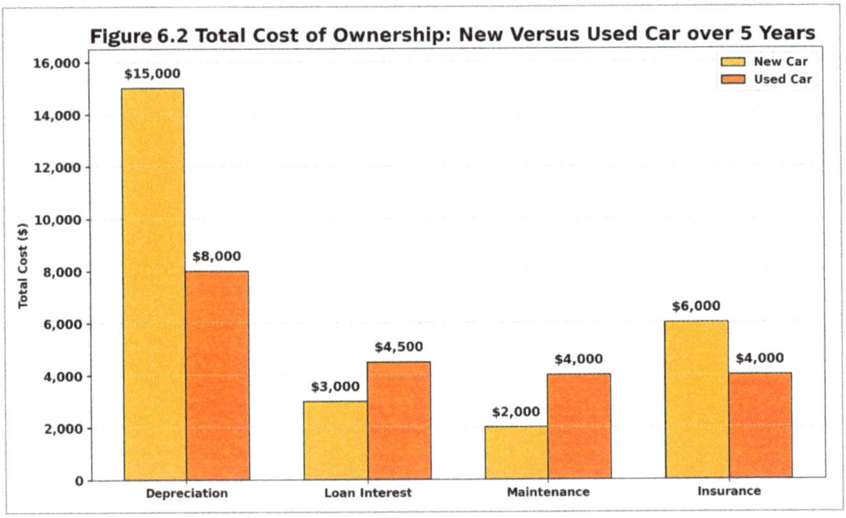

Figure 6.2 Source: Your Blueprint for Financial Literacy

Do You Finance a Car in the Same Way You Finance a Home?

We learned in chapter 5 that financing a home involves extensive paperwork, higher credit standards, and larger financial commitments. Cars, while also major purchases, involve a simpler process. Still, auto loans and mortgage loans share some similarities—and key differences. According to Quicken Loans, mortgage loans are far more rigorous. Although you may need a decent credit score to qualify for an auto loan, home loans often require excellent credit due to the significantly larger loan amount.

Increased credit scrutiny. Credit again plays a starring role. Mortgage lenders examine your full credit history from all three major bureaus: Equifax, Experian, and TransUnion. The lenders look for red flags like late payments, bankruptcies, and high debt loads. Michelle Black, president of the credit-repair firm HOPE4USA, explains that recent bankruptcies or foreclosures can severely hinder your chances of mortgage approval. If this happens, keep in mind that chapter 7 bankruptcy stays on your report for ten years, chapter 13 bankruptcy for seven.[111] Chapter 7 bankruptcy is a process that clears most debts by selling any property you own that isn't legally protected. Once complete, you get a fresh start. Chapter 13 bankruptcy is a plan that lets you keep your property while making smaller payments toward your debts over three to five years. These issues may also affect auto loans, but auto lenders tend to be more flexible—though this flexibility often comes with higher interest rates. Bob Lonergan of Zoot Enterprises notes, "The auto industry wants to sell more cars. They're more willing to lend to customers with imperfect credit, but those customers will pay more in interest."[112]

Paperwork requirements. Whether you're applying for a mortgage or a car loan, be prepared to verify your income, assets, and insurance. You'll typically need to provide these items:

- Recent pay stubs

111 Black, "Heading to the Car Dealership? Get a Great Deal by Following These 9 Steps."

112 Victoria Araj, "What's the Difference Between a Mortgage and an Auto Loan?," Quicken Loans, March 8, 2024, https://www.quickenloans.com/learn/whats-the-difference-between-a-mortgage-and-an-auto-loan.

- Tax returns
- Bank statements
- Proof of insurance (auto or homeowners')

While mortgage approval may take thirty to forty-five days, an auto loan can often be finalized the same day. Still, getting preapproved by a bank or credit union before visiting a dealership could help you secure better terms.

Pro tip—always compare interest rates and loan terms. A small difference in rates can lead to thousands of dollars saved over the life of your loan.

Refer to table 6.1 for a comparison of auto loans and mortgage loans to help illustrate the key differences in credit requirements, paperwork, approval timelines, and overall financial impact.

Auto Loan versus Mortgage Loan Comparison (2023)

Category	**Auto Loan (2023)**	**Mortgage Loan (2023)**
Typical Loan Amount	\$25,000–\$40,000	\$200,000–\$500,000+
Approval Time	Same day to 1 week	30–45 days
Credit Score Requirement	580+ (flexible)	620+ (stricter)
Interest Rate (Avg.)	6.5%–9.0%	6.75%–7.25%
Loan Term	3–7 years	15–30 years
Paperwork Required	Moderate	Extensive
Impact of Bad Credit	Higher rate, but still approved	May lead to denial

Table 6.1 Source: Your Blueprint for Financial Literacy

Do I Need a Down Payment?

The quick answer? Technically, no—but it comes at a cost. According to Investopedia, if you need a car but don't have the cash for a down payment, many lenders will still approve you to finance the entire amount.[113] But there's a catch: You'll likely pay for that convenience through a much higher interest rate. Still, there are a few ways to make a no-money-down deal more manageable.

Bring a cosigner. A family member or friend with strong credit can help you qualify for a better rate. But proceed with caution; if you miss payments, it can hurt both your credit and theirs. And don't be surprised if your cosigner starts acting like the car is half theirs.

Boost your credit score. Lenders offer better terms to borrowers who have a stable income, a consistent residence history, and—yes—*good credit.* A score of 680 or higher gives you the best shot at avoiding sky-high rates. If your score falls between 580 and 669, you may still get approved but expect higher monthly costs. If you have a lower score (below 580), approval becomes very difficult without either a cosigner or a higher income.

Negotiating helps. If you're in a strong job situation and have a clean credit report, don't hesitate to negotiate. Show that you're a reliable borrower even without up-front cash.

Save a little. This is the smarter route. The more money you can put down, the better your chances of securing a favorable interest rate—and saving thousands over the life of your loan.

Reminder—even a small down payment can reduce your interest, shorten your loan term, and increase your equity right from the start. If possible, waiting and saving is usually worth the effort.

113 Leah Zitter, "Here's How to Get a Car with No Down Payment," Investopedia, April 7, 2023, https://www.investopedia.com/articles/company-insights/083016/heres-how-get-car-no-down-payment.asp.

Figure 6.3 illustrates estimated auto loan APRs based on credit score, comparing rates with and without a down payment.

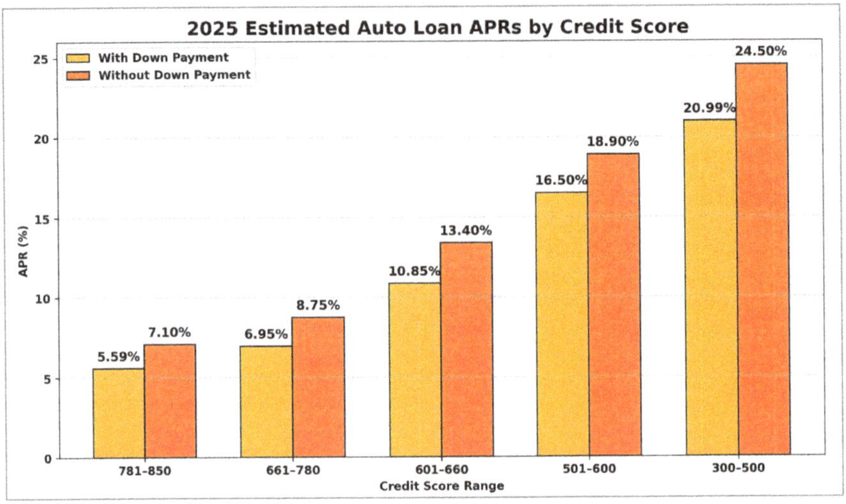

Figure 6.3 Source: Your Blueprint for Financial Literacy

What's a Car Warranty?

A car warranty is one of the most important aspects to consider when buying a vehicle. Unfortunately, not all vehicles are covered by warranties, especially used cars—and even new-car warranties come with limitations. According to NerdWallet, most new vehicles come with manufacturer warranties that cover the cost of repairs due to manufacturing defects for a limited time.[114] Additionally, you can purchase extended warranties to cover repairs after the original warranty expires. A car warranty is essentially a contract: The manufacturer or warranty provider agrees to cover specific repairs for a designated period. For example, if your vehicle's air conditioning fails due to a manufacturer defect, the warranty may cover the repair cost. However, the warranty doesn't cover issues from driver

114 Funto Omojola, "What Is a Car Warranty?," NerdWallet, updated November 19, 2025, https://www.nerdwallet.com/article/loans/auto-loans/what-is-a-car-warranty.

misuse or regular wear and tear. Most manufacturer warranties last for three years or thirty-six thousand miles, whichever comes first.[115]

Tip—car warranties typically transfer with ownership. If you're buying a used vehicle, check the original purchase date and mileage to see if the warranty still applies or if it is transferable. Extended warranties can also be purchased for used vehicles.

Several types of warranties are common:[116]

Bumper-to-bumper, also known as a **comprehensive warranty**, covers most parts between a vehicle's front and rear bumpers, including the HVAC system, electronics, and steering. It excludes maintenance services and wear and tear items. Standard coverage is three years or thirty-six thousand miles.

Powertrain covers parts that power the car, such as the engine, transmission, and drivetrain. The powertrain warranty usually lasts longer than the bumper-to-bumper warranty. For example, Honda's powertrain warranty is five years or thirty-six thousand miles, while Hyundai offers ten years or a hundred thousand miles.

An **extended** warranty is extra coverage you can buy to help pay for repairs after the manufacturer's warranty runs out. It can save you money if big repairs pop up.

Note that service contracts are sometimes marketed as extended warranties. However, they don't meet the federal definition of a warranty and may include routine maintenance services.

During college, I experienced a repair issue with my car's CV boots.

115 Omojola,"What Is a Car Warranty?"

116 Omojola,"What Is a Car Warranty?"

It was explained to me by the mechanic that CV boots are rubber covers that keep the joints by your wheels clean and greased. If one cracks, dirt gets in, the grease leaks out, and before long, you're looking at a costly repair. I'd purchased an extended warranty, which the dealership initially overlooked. After realizing the car was covered, the service department was less than pleased because warranties limit the use of new parts and dictate labor rates. This incident reminded me how valuable a warranty can be when expensive repairs come up unexpectedly.

Less Common Warranties

- **Roadside assistance** typically includes tows, tire changes, and emergency services. Although this warranty is convenient, check if your auto insurance already offers this coverage before purchasing separately.
- A **corrosion warranty**, also called a rust warranty, covers repairs to sheet metal parts damaged by corrosion.
- **Federal emissions warranties** ensure that repairs are made to components that help your car meet federal Environmental Protection Agency emission standards.

Car warranties provide peace of mind, but they are not one size fits all. Always evaluate whether the coverage matches your vehicle's age and reliability plus your ability to handle unexpected repair costs out of pocket.

Should I Buy or Lease; What's the Difference?

When I returned to New York City from London, my first car purchase in the US wasn't really a purchase at all—it was a **lease**. At the time, I'd just started a new job and didn't want the financial burden of a long-term auto loan until I felt secure in my new role. Leasing offered a low-commitment option, and I was able to drive a new car with manageable monthly payments.

Everyone has an opinion on leasing versus buying, but Edmunds.com offers a well-rounded comparison.[117] Although buying a car typically leads to greater long-term savings, leasing may be the better option for those focused on lower up-front costs, lower maintenance obligations, and access to newer vehicles with the latest features.

What Is Leasing?

Leasing a car is similar to renting: You agree to drive the vehicle for a set period (typically two to four years) with specific terms and conditions. Although it may offer a lower monthly payment, you won't own the car at the end of the lease. You'll also need to stay within an annual mileage cap—commonly twelve thousand to fifteen thousand miles—or pay overage fees. If you expect to exceed those limits, some leasing companies allow you to prepay for extra mileage, usually between ten cents and thirty cents per mile. If you drive frequently or over long distances, buying may be a smarter long-term investment. High mileage reduces a car's resale value and increases wear and tear, which could also result in lease-end fees.[118]

Pros and Cons of Leasing a Car

Pros

- Monthly payments may be lower.
- You may have minimal or no down payment.
- Maintenance costs are lower.

117 Ronald Montoya, "Leasing vs. Buying a Car: Which Is Better for You?," Edmunds, December 1, 2020, https://www.edmunds.com/car-leasing/should-you-lease-or-buy-your-car.html.

118 Montoya, "Leasing vs. Buying a Car: Which Is Better for You?"

- Depreciation is not your concern.
- Credit score requirements are lower.

Cons

- You don't own the car.
- Modifications are prohibited.
- Mileage restrictions apply.
- You may owe wear and tear charges.
- Lease-end fees may apply.
- You must maintain the car per the agreement.
- A security deposit may be required.

Pros and Cons of Buying a Car

Pros

- You gain full ownership.
- You'll have no car payments once the loan is paid.
- You may customize the vehicle.
- Mileage or lease penalties do not apply.

Cons

- Monthly payments are higher.
- Up-front costs are more expensive.
- The car's value depreciates over time.
- You are responsible for full maintenance.

Common Leasing Fees to Expect

Whether at the beginning, middle, or end of your lease, you may face several types of fees:[119]

- **Acquisition** or **administrative fees** are charged by the leasing company to initiate the lease.
- **Dealer documentation fees** cover paperwork and processing.
- **Destination** and **handling fees** are the delivery charges included in most leases.
- **Monthly rental fees** cover your agreed lease payment.
- **Disposition** or **turn-in fees** are charged when returning the car.
- **Early termination fees** apply if you end the lease before its term.

Tip—leasing can be ideal for those who prioritize flexibility and low up-front cost. Buying is best for those who drive long distances, want equity, and plan to keep the car for many years.

Figure 6.4 is a comparison chart illustrating the estimated costs of leasing versus buying a car over a three-year period, highlighting key categories such as total payments, down payments, repairs, and ownership equity.

119 Chase Bank, "Understanding the Costs of Leasing a Car," Chase Auto Education, accessed August 25, 2025, https://www.chase.com/personal/auto/education/leasing/cost-of-leasing-a-car.

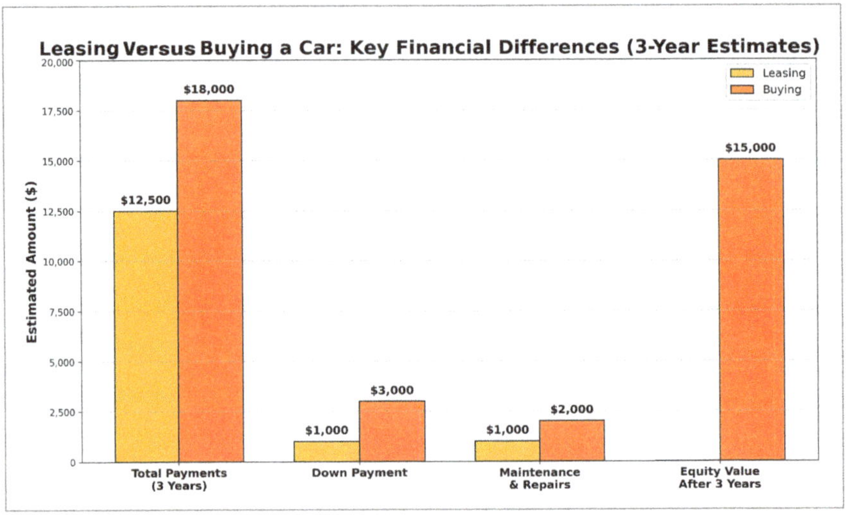

Figure 6.4 Source: Your Blueprint for Financial Literacy

What Fees Are Associated with Buying a Car?

When buying a car, especially through a dealership, understanding the full breakdown of fees can help prevent surprises and unnecessary expenses. While some charges are legitimate and required by law, others are negotiable or avoidable with the right preparation.[120] Table 6.2 lists common car-dealer fees you should know about.

Table 6.2. Car-Dealer Fees: What to Expect and What You Can Negotiate

Fee Type	Description	Negotiable
Title and registration	Covers registering your vehicle with the state DMV and issuing the license plate. Often handled by the dealer.	✗ Not typically

120 Louis DeNicola, "Dealer Fees You Should Know When Buying a Car," Credit Karma, November 8, 2024, https://www.creditkarma.com/auto/i/dealer-fees-buying-car.

Fee Type	Description	Negotiable
Sales tax	Based on the state or municipality. Some states deduct your trade-in value from the sales price before calculating sales tax.	✗ No
Destination charge	Fee to transport the car from the factory to the dealership. Applies to new cars, even if you pick it up from the factory.	✗ No
Documentation fee	Dealer's processing cost for paperwork. Varies widely by state and dealer.	✓ Sometimes
Advertising fee	Dealers may try to pass along regional or local advertising costs.	✓ Sometimes
Dealer prep fee	Charges for cleaning and preparing a new vehicle.	✓ Often
Transport fees (additional)	Applies if a specific car needs to be delivered from another dealership.	✓ Sometimes
Extended warranties	Optional coverage sold by the dealer beyond the manufacturer's warranty.	✓ Yes
Maintenance plans	Prepaid service packages for routine maintenance.	✓ Yes
VIN etching	Engraving the VIN on windows for theft deterrence. DIY kits are available for much less.	✓ Yes
Credit insurance	Optional insurance that covers your auto loan if you lose your job, become disabled, or pass away.	✓ Yes
GAP insurance	Covers the difference between the loan balance and car value if your vehicle is totaled. Mandatory for leases; optional when buying.	✓ Sometimes

Table 6.2 Source: Your Blueprint for Financial Literacy

Do I Need Auto Insurance?

The short answer is yes. If you have a vehicle that is driven by you or someone else, and it's registered with your state's DMV, some form of auto insurance is generally required. As the vehicle owner, your responsibility is to determine the type and amount of coverage that best fits your needs. According to Forbes Advisor, every state has a minimum level of car insurance you must carry to meet financial responsibility laws.[121] As discussed in chapter 4, liability insurance is the most common required coverage. It pays for damage or injuries you cause to others in an accident. However, requirements vary by state, so understanding your specific state laws is key. The National Association of Insurance Commissioners recommends carrying enough coverage to

- Comply with your state's insurance laws,
- Satisfy any requirements from a lender (if you're financing or leasing), and
- Protect your personal financial assets.[122]

While most states mandate liability insurance, others require additional coverage types, such as **uninsured motorist protection** or **personal injury protection**. If you're leasing or financing, your lender will likely require **collision** and **comprehensive coverage** as well.

States That Don't Require Auto Insurance (as of 2024)[123]

- New Hampshire doesn't require insurance, but you must prove you can cover costs if you're at fault in an accident.

121 Penny Gusner, "How Much Car Insurance Do I Need?," Forbes Advisor, accessed November 13, 2024, https://www.forbes.com/advisor/car-insurance/how-much-car-insurance-do-you-need/.

122 Gusner, "How Much Car Insurance Do I Need?"

123 Gusner, "How Much Car Insurance Do I Need?"

- South Carolina allows uninsured driving if you meet certain qualifications and pay a $600 registration fee.

How to Find the Right Coverage

To get the best rate, compare quotes from multiple insurers. Your age, vehicle type, location, driving history, and credit score all affect premiums. At a minimum, you should meet your state's requirements—but ideally, you want coverage that fully protects you and your vehicle.

Types of Auto Insurance Coverage

As discussed in chapter 4, these are the most common types of auto insurance:[124]

- Liability insurance covers injuries or property damage you cause others in an accident. It also includes your legal defense if you're sued.
  - ✓ Bodily injury liability covers medical costs for other parties.
  - ✓ Property damage liability pays for damage to someone else's vehicle or property.
- Uninsured or underinsured motorist coverage protects you if another driver has little or no insurance.
  - ✓ Medical expenses for you and passengers
  - ✓ Lost wages
  - ✓ Funeral costs
  - ✓ Pain and suffering
  - ✓ Vehicle repairs (depending on state)

124 Gusner, "How Much Car Insurance Do I Need?"

  - Note that the at-fault, uninsured driver receives no benefit under this coverage.

- Personal injury protection pays for your and your passengers' medical expenses, lost income, and essential services—regardless of fault. This is required in some states.
- Medical payments coverage is similar to personal injury protection but with limited coverage. It pays for medical costs from an accident, regardless of fault and is required in states like Pennsylvania, Maine, and New Hampshire.
- GAP insurance covers the difference between your vehicle's actual value and the amount you owe on your loan or lease if the car is totaled or stolen. I once had a vehicle stolen, and gap insurance saved me thousands.
- Rental reimbursement covers the cost of a rental car or public transit while your car is being repaired due to a covered incident.
- Roadside assistance helps cover expenses if your car breaks down. Typical services include tows, jump starts, lockout assistance, and fuel delivery. Some plans also include **arrest bond coverage** for traffic violations, **legal defense reimbursement**, and **trip interruption coverage** for lodging and travel expenses if your car breaks down midtrip.

Auto insurance is more than a legal requirement—it's a safeguard that protects you from life's unexpected turns. No matter how you own your vehicle, having the right coverage gives you the freedom to focus on the road ahead with confidence and peace of mind.

CHAPTER 6 KEY TAKEAWAYS

You should now have a better understanding of the following:

- ✓ **Decision-making framework.** Gaining clarity on whether you really need a car helps you avoid or eliminate unnecessary expenses.
- ✓ **Financial comparisons.** Information on buying new versus used cars, financing options, and the importance of down payments will guide you in making informed purchases.
- ✓ **Vehicle warranties.** You've learned about car warranties and the differences between buying and leasing, helping you choose the best option for your situation.
- ✓ **Insurance necessities.** Knowledge of the requirements for auto insurance will prepare you for the responsibilities of car ownership.

Source: Your Blueprint for Financial Literacy

Chapter 7

Now That I Have a Job, What Taxes Do I Have to Pay?

As I mentioned in the preface, my first real job was at Big Bear Super Foods. I was about sixteen or seventeen years old. That summer, I spent my days walking from business to business, asking if they had any jobs I could do. I didn't know what a résumé was, nor did I have any interviewing skills. I simply knew I wanted to work and earn money. Most mornings, I would hitch a ride with my cousin Regina M. King, who would drop me off at Aunt Little Bit's house. After a long day pounding the pavement in the hot sun, I'd wait outside Regina's office for my ride home. She had no idea how instrumental she was in shaping the person I've become.

One particularly hot summer day, I stopped by Big Bear Super Foods to make my usual inquiry, and I walked in at just the right time. Shell Henson, the owner of Big Bear, was usually stocking milk or juice or tidying up canned goods somewhere in the store. I spotted him and asked once again, "Do you have any jobs?"

He paused, looked at me, pushed his hair back, and said, "When can you start?"

My eyes lit up! My cousin Joseph Shepard Jr.—nicknamed "Side" because he always walked with his head tilted to the side—used to work there. What's important to know about Side is that not only did he work at Big Bear, but he was also Aunt Little Bit's great-grandson. Back then, it was required to wear a tie while working in the supermarket. I ran straight to Aunt Little Bit's house and told her the good news. She immediately called Side and told him to bring over one of his Sunday neckties. I started working that very same day and stayed there through high school, thanks to a work-study program.

Some of you, like me, may get your first job during high school. Others may start working after college or trade school. Some of you may be immigrants landing your first job in the United States. And others may be transitioning from military to civilian life. No matter your path, one thing we'll all have in common is this: Once you start working, you'll also start paying income taxes. Let's go through some of those taxes so you can understand what they are, what they mean, and how they'll affect your paycheck.

Q&A SESSION

What Are Payroll and Income Taxes?

According to Investopedia, **income tax**, also known as **personal income tax**, is the most common type of federal tax.[125] It's based on wages, salaries, bonuses, tips, and other forms of income earned by individuals. Most states have their own income tax in addition to the federal tax. However, not everyone pays tax on the full amount of what they earn. That's because the Internal Revenue Service (IRS) allows deductions and credits, which help lower your taxable income or the amount of tax you owe.

- A **deduction** reduces your taxable income.
- A **credit** directly reduces your total tax bill.

For example, if you made $100,000 last year, and you qualify for $20,000 in deductions, you'd only be taxed on $80,000. The IRS

125 Julia Kagan, "What Is Income Tax and How Are Different Types Calculated?," Investopedia, June 24, 2024, https://www.investopedia.com/terms/i/incometax.asp.

allows deductions for things like healthcare costs, retirement investments, and education expenses.

Business income tax. If you run a business—whether you're self-employed, own a small business, or operate as a partnership or corporation—you'll need to pay taxes on the income your business earns. Just as with personal income tax, deductions are available for eligible business expenses, which can help reduce your tax bill.

State and local income taxes. Most, but not all, states in the US collect their own income taxes. At the time of writing this book in 2024, the following states *didn't* collect personal income tax:

- Alaska
- Florida
- Nevada
- South Dakota
- Tennessee
- Texas
- Washington
- Wyoming

New Hampshire also doesn't tax wages, but it currently collects tax on interest and dividends. However, that 5% tax was scheduled to phase out starting January 1, 2024.[126]

Keep in mind that just because a state doesn't charge income tax doesn't necessarily mean it's cheaper to live there. These states often raise revenue in other ways, such as through higher sales taxes, property taxes, or reduced public services. For example, Florida has a state sales tax of 6%, and Tennessee's is even higher at 7%.[127] So,

126 Kagan, "What Is Income Tax and How Are Different Types Calculated?"

127 Kagan, "What Is Income Tax and How Are Different Types Calculated?"

when deciding where to live or work, it's important to consider the full picture, including healthcare costs, job opportunities, and overall cost of living, not just the presence or absence of income taxes.

What's a Federal Income Tax, and What's a State Income Tax?

In its simplest form, tax withholding is an estimate of how much you'll owe the government at the end of the year, based on your income and other relevant factors. That estimated annual tax amount is divided across the number of pay periods you have. For example, if you are paid weekly and expect to owe $10,000 in taxes for the year, then approximately $192.30 would be withheld from each paycheck ($10,000 ÷ 52 weeks).[128]

Hourly employees may have this calculation done based on the number of hours they work during each pay period. Although both state and federal governments can withhold income taxes, the primary difference lies in the jurisdiction and tax rates being applied: Federal taxes follow a consistent national structure, while state tax rules vary depending on where you live.

Let's look at some of the differences.[129]

Federal Withholding Tax

The modern system of **federal income tax** withholding began in the 1940s to help finance World War II. Instead of paying all taxes in one lump sum each year, this system allows employers to withhold a portion of your paycheck regularly and submit it to the government on your behalf. This helps prevent the financial shock of paying a large tax bill all at once and ensures steady revenue for government services.

Here's how it works: When you begin a job, you complete IRS **Form W-4**, where you report your marital status and the number of dependents or allowances. Your employer then uses

128 Kagan, "What Is Income Tax and How Are Different Types Calculated?"

129 Kagan, "What Is Income Tax and How Are Different Types Calculated?"

this information to calculate how much federal tax to withhold from each paycheck. If you have too much withheld, you'll likely receive a refund after filing your tax return. If too little is withheld, you may owe taxes.

Some individuals, myself included, prefer to have extra withheld during the year to avoid owing anything when tax season arrives. Just make sure to confirm with your payroll department that your W-4 adjustments have been applied properly. Always check your pay stub for accuracy. To get a detailed look at a Form W-4, go to 2025 Form W-4 in your search browser.

State Withholding Tax

Just like the federal government, many state governments collect income taxes and require employers to withhold a portion of wages. However, the structure and rates vary from state to state. Some states follow a flat rate, while others use a progressive system similar to federal taxes. Again, there are nine states that do not collect personal income taxes at all, which means no state tax will be withheld from your paycheck if you live and work in these states:

- Alaska
- Florida
- Nevada
- New Hampshire
- South Dakota
- Tennessee
- Texas
- Washington
- Wyoming

Note that some of these states still impose taxes on specific types of income. For instance, Washington has a capital gains tax, and New Hampshire taxes interest and dividends.

Table 7.1. Key Differences Between Federal and State Tax Withholding

Key Differences	Federal Withholding	State Withholding
Tax Authority	IRS	State tax agencies
Consistency	Same across U.S.	Varies by state
Tax Brackets	Progressive (10%–37%)	Flat or progressive (varies)
Social Security Tax	6.2% up to annual wage limit	Not applicable
Medicare Tax	1.45% + 0.9% over $200k	Not applicable
Form Used by Employees	W-4	State-specific forms
Purpose	Funds federal programs	Funds state services

Table 7.1 Source: Your Blueprint for Financial Literacy

What Happens If No Federal Tax Is Withheld?

If no federal income tax is being deducted from your paycheck, something may be wrong—especially if you're not exempt. Exemptions are typically based on income level or certain personal situations, but most people are subject to federal tax. Withholding is designed to match, as closely as possible, what you'll actually owe at the end of the year. That way you avoid a large bill or an overly large refund. Your goal should be balance.[130]

Both state and federal withholdings are designed to help manage your tax obligation throughout the year. If too little is withheld, you may owe taxes. If too much is withheld, you'll likely receive a refund. Whether it's for Social Security, Medicare, or general income tax,

130 Sean Ross, "Federal Withholding Tax vs. State Withholding Tax: What's the Difference?," Investopedia, November 22, 2024, https://www.investopedia.com/ask/answers/051515/what-difference-between-federal-and-state-withholding-tax.asp.

understanding how withholding works can help you better manage your finances and avoid surprises at tax time.

What's a Social Security Income Tax?

Social Security tax is governed by federal law and is collected through two primary mechanisms: the **Federal Insurance Contributions Act (FICA)** for employees and the **Self-Employed Contributions Act** for individuals who work for themselves. These taxes fund the benefits distributed through the Old-Age, Survivors, and Disability Insurance program—more commonly known as Social Security. The purpose of the Social Security tax is to provide income for individuals who have retired, are disabled, or have survived a deceased worker. Rather than placing contributions in an individual account for each worker, the system operates on a pay-as-you-go model, meaning that the taxes collected today are used to pay current beneficiaries.[131] As of 2024, the Social Security tax rate is 12.4%.[132] This amount is typically divided equally between employers and employees:

- 6.2% is withheld from the employee's wages.
- 6.2% is paid directly by the employer.

The tax applies to most forms of **earned income**, such as wages, salaries, and bonuses, up to a set annual income limit determined by the Social Security Administration.

For self-employed individuals, the process is slightly different. Since the IRS views them as both employer and employee, they are responsible for the *entire* 12.4% themselves. In addition, self-employed individuals must also pay the **Medicare tax**, which brings the total self-employment tax rate to 15.3% (12.4% for Social

131 Katelyn Peters, "What Is Social Security Tax? Definition, Exemptions, and Example," Investopedia, September 6, 2024, https://www.investopedia.com/terms/s/social-security-tax.asp.

132 Peters, "What Is Social Security Tax? Definition, Exemptions, and Example."

Security and 2.9% for Medicare). Fortunately, this tax is assessed on 92.35% of the individual's net earnings, offering a modest reduction in the taxable amount.[133]

Who Is Exempt from Paying Social Security Tax?

Although most workers are subject to Social Security tax, specific exemptions are available for certain individuals and groups:[134]

- Members of recognized religious sects who are conscientiously opposed to accepting Social Security benefits under any circumstances
- Nonresident aliens who are temporarily in the US on student visas and are not citizens or lawful permanent residents
- Nonresident aliens employed in the US by a foreign government
- Students working for the same educational institution in which they are enrolled, provided that their employment is directly tied to their status as a student

These exceptions are relatively narrow and require proper documentation or legal status to qualify. For most individuals working in the United States, contributing to Social Security is a mandatory part of employment or self-employment.

What's a Medicare Income Tax?

Medicare tax is a federal employment tax that helps fund a portion of the **Medicare insurance program**, specifically **Medicare Part A**, which covers hospital-related expenses. As of 2024, the Medicare tax rate is 1.45% for employees and 1.45% for employers, totaling 2.9%.

133 Peters, "What Is Social Security Tax? Definition, Exemptions, and Example."

134 Peters, "What Is Social Security Tax? Definition, Exemptions, and Example."

Like Social Security tax, Medicare tax is automatically withheld from an employee's paycheck. For individuals who are self-employed, this tax is included in their self-employment tax obligations.

Often referred to as the hospital insurance tax, the Medicare tax supports services such as inpatient hospital stays, hospice care, limited stays in skilled nursing facilities, and some forms of home healthcare. Nearly all individuals working in the United States are subject to this tax. Under FICA, employers must withhold both Social Security and Medicare taxes from employee wages. The Self-Employed Contributions Act applies the same responsibility to self-employed individuals, who must pay both the employer and employee share. Funds collected from Medicare taxes are deposited into the **Hospital Insurance Trust Fund**, which is managed by the US Treasury. These funds are used to pay for Medicare Part A services.[135]

It is important to note that **Medicare Parts B** and **D**—which cover outpatient services and prescription drug costs, respectively—*aren't funded by Medicare tax*. Instead, they're financed through the **Supplementary Medical Insurance Trust Fund**, which receives revenue from beneficiary premiums, general tax revenue, and investment income. While Medicare taxes are meant to support both current and future beneficiaries, the Hospital Insurance Trust Fund has faced financial pressure for many years. Current projections suggest that the fund may be depleted by 2031 unless reforms are implemented.[136] This may require either increased funding, benefit adjustments, or legislative changes to ensure long-term sustainability.

Unlike Social Security tax, Medicare tax doesn't have an income cap. That means all earned income—such as wages, tips, bonuses, commissions, and certain taxable benefits—is subject to the 1.45% tax rate. In 2013, the ACA introduced two additional Medicare-related taxes for high-income earners:[137]

---

135 Kathryn Flynn, "Medicare Tax: What Is It and Who Pays It?," Investopedia, January 22, 2024, https://www.investopedia.com/medicare-tax-definition-5115380.

136 Flynn, "Medicare Tax: What Is It and Who Pays It?"

137 Flynn, "Medicare Tax: What Is It and Who Pays It?"

- **Additional Medicare Tax**, which applies to wages above a specific threshold (e.g., $200,000 for single filers)
- **Net Investment Income Tax**, which applies to certain types of investment income for individuals above income limits

In some cases, a taxpayer may be liable for *both* surtaxes depending on the type and amount of income they earn.

What's a Local Tax?

Local taxes are imposed by state, county, or municipal governments to fund essential public services such as schools, emergency services, road maintenance, and sanitation. These taxes can take many forms and often vary widely depending on where a person lives.

Under the US Constitution, federal and state governments have the authority to impose taxes, and local governments—cities, towns, and counties—may also do so through what are commonly referred to as **municipal taxes.**[138]

Local taxes help fund services like these:

- Public education
- Police and fire departments
- Libraries and public health services
- Road repairs and infrastructure
- Parks and recreational programs

In many cases, local projects also receive additional support through **federal grants**.

138 Julia Kagan, "Local Tax: What It Is and Types," Investopedia, June 16, 2024, https://www.investopedia.com/terms/l/localtax.asp.

Types of Local Taxes

The amount and type of local taxes can vary, but these are common forms you may encounter.[139]

Property tax is the most common and often the largest local tax residents pay. It's typically based on the assessed value of real estate. States like New Jersey and New York have some of the highest property tax rates in the country, while Alabama is among those with the lowest.

Some states and cities impose **miscellaneous local taxes**, like a **local income tax**, which is withheld directly from employee wages. These taxes are relatively rare—only sixteen states currently allow them. In some places, like Ohio, school districts can impose an additional income tax to help cover education expenses.[140]

Sales tax is another major revenue source for local governments. It's applied to the sale of goods and services and is considered a **regressive tax** because all consumers pay the same rate regardless of income. Only five states do not impose a state-level sales tax: Alaska, Delaware, Montana, New Hampshire, and Oregon.[141] Sales tax laws are often complex. For example, some states exempt groceries or reduce the tax rate on large purchases, like vehicles. Other states impose additional taxes on certain items, such as **sin taxes** on cigarettes and alcohol. In some locations, like New York City, local sales tax is added to the state's sales tax, resulting in a higher combined rate. **Use taxes** are also common and apply to major purchases made out of state, such as vehicles, which must be taxed in the buyer's home state.

Why Local Taxes Matter

State and local governments rely heavily on these taxes to maintain the infrastructure and services their communities need to function. While federal taxes support national programs, the direct

139 Kagan, "Local Tax: What It Is and Types."

140 Kagan, "Local Tax: What It Is and Types."

141 Kagan, "Local Tax: What It Is and Types."

benefit of local taxes is often felt most immediately—whether it's the condition of your neighborhood streets or the quality of your local schools. At the same time, local governments must strike a balance. High taxes can cause public pushback, while low taxes may lead to service cutbacks, delayed repairs, or school budget cuts.

Figure 7.1 is a pay statement showing a biweekly paycheck with a blue-and-white layout. It highlights a gross pay of $3,000.00, net pay of $2,035.50, and key deductions.

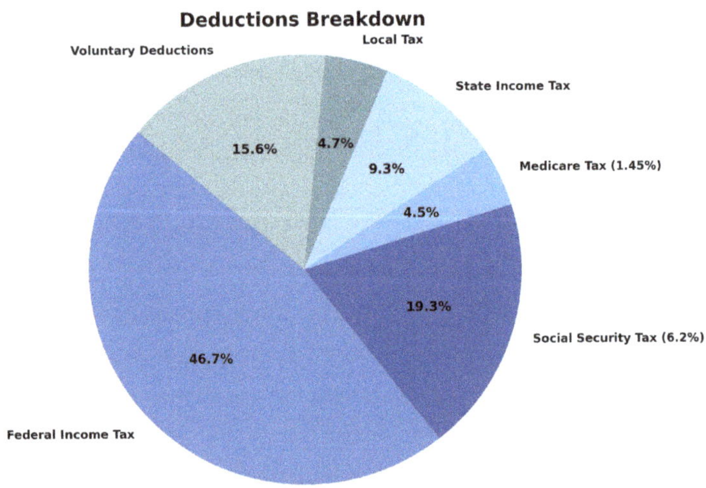

EARNINGS		DEDUCTIONS	
Gross Pay	$3,000.00	Federal Income Tax	$450.00
		Social Security Tax	$186.00
		Medicare Tax	$43.50
		State Income Tax	$90.00
		Local Tax	$45.00
		Voluntary Deductions	$150.00
GROSS PAY	$3,000.00		
NET PAY	$2,035.50		

Figure 7.1 Source: Your Blueprint for Financial Literacy

How Do I File an Income Tax Return?

January is often a month of mixed emotions. Some of us wonder how quickly the last year passed. Others feel the pressure of a new beginning. Many set goals and resolutions, although, let's be honest, a good number of them don't last past the end of the month. But one thing that does stick around and demand attention is filing your income taxes. For anyone who worked in the prior year, this becomes a reality you can't ignore. Filing taxes is more than just paperwork; it's a legal responsibility tied to your income, not something to be taken lightly. During tax season, the IRS operates at full capacity—it's about as busy as Times Square on New Year's Eve. As long as you had a paying job the previous year, you're likely required to file. And while tax preparation may seem intimidating, understanding the process helps make it much more manageable. Investopedia provides helpful insights into this process, and much of what follows is rooted in the practical advice they've shared.[142]

How to Prepare Your Taxes

There are three common methods for filing taxes:[143]

- Doing it yourself using paper or online IRS forms
- Using tax preparation software
- Hiring a professional tax preparer

If you're filing for the first time, it's a good idea to get advice or help. As you gain experience, you'll become more comfortable deciding which method is best for you.

Filing taxes manually (with paper or online forms). You can take the traditional approach and download tax forms directly from

142 Investopedia Team, "How to File Your Tax Return," Investopedia, May 4, 2025, https://www.investopedia.com/ask/answers/051415/what-are-different-ways-i-can-file-my-income-tax-return.asp.

143 Investopedia Team, "How to File Your Tax Return."

the IRS website. All federal forms are available through the IRS Forms, Instructions, and Publications Search Tool. State income tax forms are usually available on your state's official tax website. You can either print them and mail in your return or complete the forms online and file electronically. Many public libraries also have tax forms available. If you owe taxes, payment can be submitted with your return.

This approach is *free*, and while it may take more time, it also offers a chance to better understand your income, deductions, and financial habits. It's an excellent option for learning how your money flows and how taxes work.

Using tax software. Tax preparation software offers a helpful middle ground. It walks you through the steps of filing your federal and state returns, asks guided questions, and can even carry over your prior year's data. Some programs also offer live support from professionals for a fee.

Popular tax software platforms include TurboTax, H&R Block, TaxAct, and Jackson Hewitt. These tools are ideal for individuals who want a user-friendly experience without hiring a professional, especially if their financial situation is relatively straightforward.

Hiring a tax professional. For people with more complex finances—like rental property owners, freelancers, or those who earn income across multiple states—hiring a tax preparer may be the best route. Experienced professionals help reduce the risk of errors, identify valuable deductions, and ensure your return is accurate and compliant. Personally, as my tax situation became more complicated, I found professionals to be a wise investment. One year, I had to file returns in three states. That's when I fully appreciated the benefit of having someone who knows the tax code inside and out.

Still, it's important to remember that while a preparer assists with filing, *you are legally responsible* for what's submitted. Be sure to choose someone reputable.

Documents You'll Need to File Your Taxes

Regardless of the filing method you choose, the first step is gathering your documentation. You'll need to report your filing status, income, taxes already paid, and any deductions or credits. Most tax-related forms are sent out by the end of January. Here's a breakdown of what you'll need, based on your employment and personal circumstances.[144]

General Information

- Full names
- Birth dates
- Social Security numbers

You'll need these general information items for yourself, your spouse, and your dependents.[145]

Income Documents

- **W-2 form**, provided by your employer, reports income and withholdings
- **1099-NEC**, provided by clients if you earned $600 or more from contract work or freelance jobs
- **1099-MISC**, received if you earned $600 or more in rent, prize money, or other miscellaneous income
- **1099-INT**, provided by banks or institutions if you earned over ten dollars in interest
- Documentation of **IRA contributions** (traditional and Roth)

144 Investopedia Team, "How to File Your Tax Return."

145 Investopedia Team, "How to File Your Tax Return."

If you plan to itemize deductions instead of taking the standard deduction, you'll need to provide these items:

- Mortgage interest and property taxes, typically reported on **Form 1098**
- Separate records of property tax payments, especially if not paid through escrow
- Proof of state and local taxes paid, usually on your W-2 or through quarterly payments for contractors
- Records of charitable donations
- Documentation of qualified education expenses, such as tuition and student fees
- Receipts for unreimbursed medical expenses, which are only deductible if they exceed 7.5% of AGI
- Copies of last year's federal and state tax returns

That car I once donated to National Public Radio? That's the kind of charitable gift that qualifies for a tax deduction—subject to limits based on your adjusted gross income (AGI). Remember those high-yield savings accounts we discussed earlier? That interest may seem small, but it's taxable income. That "free money" comes with strings attached.

What's the Quickest Way to Get a Tax Refund?

Step 1 is to file early before a backlog builds up at the IRS. Step 2 is to file electronically; these returns are processed more quickly, and you can generally get your refund in fewer than twenty-one days. It can take six months to process a return sent on paper, according to the IRS.[146]

146 Investopedia Team, "How to File Your Tax Return."

Is It Better to File Electronically or to Mail in a Paper Tax Return?

Filing your tax return electronically is always better and faster.[147] Be sure to take advantage of IRS protections, such as Identity Protection PINs, and establish multifactor authentication if you do your taxes using an online provider. I would advise you, as a beginner, to work with someone more knowledgeable before going at it alone. Be careful. I once had a person tell me that my work suits could count as uniform deductions, and that simply wasn't true. You will be required to sign the finished forms stating that all the information you are filing is true. This means you are held accountable for misinformation on your taxes. Filing inaccurate tax forms could lead to audits and fines.

147 Investopedia Team, "How to File Your Tax Return."

CHAPTER 7 KEY TAKEAWAYS

You should now have a better understanding of the following:

- ✓ **Tax literacy.** Knowledge of the various taxes that apply to your income and location will help you budget accurately and choose the appropriate withholding amounts for your paycheck.
- ✓ **Filing knowledge.** Guidance on how to file income tax returns will equip you to manage your tax responsibilities accurately.

Source: Your Blueprint for Financial Literacy

Chapter 8

Now That I Have a Job, How Do I Save For Retirement?

Retirement is a word you're likely to hear long before you actually enter the workforce. Every day, thousands of people retire, stepping away from their careers permanently. In simple terms, *retirement* means leaving your occupation and not returning to it in a work capacity. In the United States, traditional retirement begins between the ages of sixty-two and sixty-five, although some people retire earlier or later depending on their financial readiness, health, or personal goals.

People look forward to retirement for different reasons. Some are simply exhausted from decades of working. Others want the freedom to travel or spend more time with family but can't do so during their working years because of job demands or financial limitations.

The concept of preparing for retirement is not unique to the United States. Around the world, people are thinking about how to sustain themselves once they stop earning a paycheck. For most of us, this means building financial resources now to support our future selves later in life. Back in 2016, I started to take this seriously. I realized that I wasn't on track to retire comfortably, and that realization made me pause. I didn't want to reach retirement age and find myself unprepared. So, I made the decision to act.

There are multiple ways to prepare for retirement financially, and several factors can influence your retirement strategy. For example, where you live and your lifestyle choices can play a significant role in how much money you'll need. This chapter will offer you a starting point. Whether retirement feels as if it's decades away or just around the corner, now is always the right time to begin planning. Some of the topics covered may be completely new to you, regardless of your age. That's okay—retirement planning is rarely taught, even though it falls directly under the umbrella of home economics and personal finance.

Ultimately, your retirement is your responsibility. No one else is going to prepare for it on your behalf. How you plan today will determine how financially secure and confident you feel when the time comes.

Q&A SESSION

What's a Retirement Plan?

According to Investopedia, early retirement generally begins at age sixty-two, which is also the earliest age you can start collecting Social Security retirement benefits.[148] However, keep in mind that collecting early means receiving reduced benefits for the rest of your life. We touched on Social Security in a previous chapter, and as a reminder—full retirement age is considered sixty-seven for those born in 1960 or later.[149] The amount you receive in benefits depends largely on how much you paid into the system during your working years.

Social Security typically replaces about 40% of your pre-retirement income, so it's not designed to be your only source of support. You'll need to supplement it with other savings or income. Planning how much you'll need in total retirement income starts with estimating your expected Social Security benefits, then figuring out how much more you'll need to maintain your lifestyle. On average, most people live fifteen to twenty years after age sixty-five, but many live longer.[150] That means your retirement

148 Julia Kagan, "Definition of Retirement and Tips for How to Save, Plan, and Invest," Investopedia, July 18, 2024, https://www.investopedia.com/terms/r/retirement.asp.

149 Kagan, "Definition of Retirement and Tips for How to Save, Plan, and Invest."

150 Kagan, "Definition of Retirement and Tips for How to Save, Plan, and Invest."

savings may need to last *two decades or more.* A good rule of thumb is that most retirees will need around 80% of their pre-retirement income to maintain their current standard of living.[151]

When developing a retirement plan, consider these factors:[152]

- Your target retirement age
- The **cost of living** and how it may rise over time (**inflation**)
- The value of your current savings and investments
- A realistic rate of return on your investments
- The estimated value of your Social Security and **pension** (if applicable)
- Where you plan to live after you retire

Don't forget, inflation reduces your purchasing power over time. Even a modest inflation rate of 3% to 4% annually can affect your retirement income significantly. Adjust your savings plan accordingly. Starting early offers the biggest advantage. But if you're getting a late start, don't panic. There are still ways to catch up. According to Investopedia and other financial experts, keys to retirement success include the following:[153]

- Choosing investments based on your risk tolerance and time horizon
- Diversifying your portfolio to reduce risk
- Setting up automatic transfers from your bank account into your retirement fund

151 Kagan, "Definition of Retirement and Tips for How to Save, Plan, and Invest."

152 Kagan, "Definition of Retirement and Tips for How to Save, Plan, and Invest."

153 Kagan, "Definition of Retirement and Tips for How to Save, Plan, and Invest."

- Contributing as much as possible to your employer -sponsored plan
- Reducing or eliminating high-interest debt

It's never too late to start saving for retirement. Those who begin later may need to tighten their budgets and increase their contributions, but reaching your goals is still possible with commitment and planning.

What's a 401(k), and How Do I Get One?

A 401(k) is an employer-sponsored retirement plan that allows you to contribute a portion of your income to a retirement investment account.[154] Many employers offer to match part of your contributions, which is essentially free money toward your retirement.

There are two main types of 401(k) plans: traditional and Roth. With a **traditional 401(k)**, contributions are made *before* taxes, which lowers your taxable income now, but withdrawals during retirement are taxed. With a **Roth 401(k)**, contributions are made *after* taxes. There's no tax break today, but withdrawals in retirement are tax-free if certain conditions are met. If your employer offers either plan, I strongly recommend taking advantage of it. When you enroll, you choose a percentage of your paycheck to be automatically invested.[155]

Investopedia recommends the following steps when setting up your 401(k):[156]

- Ask your employer if they offer a plan and if there's a **company match**.
- Once enrolled, choose your investment options—ranging from conservative to aggressive. A common choice is a

154 Jason Fernando, "401(k) Plans: What Are They, How They Work," Investopedia, January 24, 2025, https://www.investopedia.com/terms/1/401kplan.asp.

155 Fernando, "401(k) Plans: What Are They, How They Work."

156 Fernando, "401(k) Plans: What Are They, How They Work."

target-date fund, which adjusts risk levels based on your expected retirement year.

- If you're self-employed, you might qualify for a **solo 401(k)**, available through many online brokers.

Contribution Limits as of 2024

- Employee limit (under age fifty): $23,000
- Catch-up (age fifty and up): an additional $7,500
- Total combined employee and employer limit
  - Under age fifty: $69,000
  - Age fifty and up: $76,500

You can contribute to both traditional and Roth 401(k) plans, as long as your combined contributions don't exceed the annual limit.

How Your 401(k) Grows. Your contributions are invested in options offered by your employer—usually **mutual funds**, **bonds**, and target-date funds. Growth depends on several factors:[157]

- How much you contribute
- Company matches
- Investment performance
- Time until retirement

One major advantage is **tax-deferred growth** for traditional 401(k)s or **tax-free growth** for Roth 401(k)s. The earlier you start, the more you benefit from compounding, where your earnings

157 Fernando, "401(k) Plans: What Are They, How They Work."

generate their own earnings over time.[158]

Withdrawals and taxes. For traditional 401(k)s, withdrawals are taxed as income. For Roth 401(k)s, qualified withdrawals are tax-free. You must be at least fifty-nine and a half, or meet certain IRS conditions, to avoid penalties. **Early withdrawals** may face a 10% penalty, in addition to regular taxes.[159] Some plans allow 401(k) loans, but if you leave your job, the loan often becomes immediately due.

Required minimum distributions. For traditional 401(k)s, **required minimum distributions (RMDs)** begin at age seventy-three. The amount is based on your life expectancy. The rules regarding RMDs were updated under the 2022 omnibus spending bill (H.R. 2617).[160]

Roth 401(k)s are also subject to RMDs, unlike Roth IRAs, which are not.

401(k)s versus brokerage accounts. Although I contribute to a 401(k) through my employer, I also have a Roth IRA. I personally favor a **brokerage account** for its flexibility.

Table 8.1 shows some of the differences between 401(k)s and brokerage accounts:

158 Fernando, "401(k) Plans: What Are They, How They Work."

159 Fernando, "401(k) Plans: What Are They, How They Work."

160 Fernando, "401(k) Plans: What Are They, How They Work."

Table 8.1. 401(k) Versus Brokerage Accounts

Feature	401(k)	Brokerage Account
Purpose	Retirement	Any financial goal
Tax treatment	Tax-deferred or tax-free	Taxable gains and dividends
Contribution limits	Yes (e.g., $23,000 in 2024)	No contribution limits
Withdrawal rules	Age-based and penalties	No restrictions
Investment options	Employer-defined	Full market access
RMDs	Yes (except Roth IRAs)	No RMDs

Table 8.1 Source: Your Blueprint for Financial Literacy

Brokerage accounts don't offer the same tax advantages, but they give you more freedom and investment choices. They're especially helpful if your employer doesn't offer a retirement plan.

What Happens to Your 401(k) When You Leave a Job?

This is a critical topic to understand. Over the years, I've changed jobs for a variety of reasons—some by choice, others not. I've been laid off, accepted better opportunities, and even worked for companies that eventually closed their doors. The point is that things happen, and not all of them are within your control as an employee. Still, when you leave a job, you have several options when it comes to your 401(k). I've used a few of these myself over time. Let's break down your choices:[161]

Withdraw the money. Taking a direct withdrawal from your 401(k) is usually the *least recommended option*, unless you're in urgent need.

- You'll owe income tax on the amount you take out.
- You'll likely face a 10% **early-withdrawal penalty** unless

161 Fernando, "401(k) Plans: What Are They, How They Work."

you're over fifty-nine and a half, permanently disabled, or qualified for another IRS exemption.

- For a Roth 401(k), you can withdraw your contributions (not earnings) tax-free if the account is at least five years old.

Even with those allowances, early withdrawals reduce your future savings—and that can be hard to recover from.

Roll over your 401(k) into an IRA. This is one of the most popular and tax-smart options. You can transfer your balance into an **IRA** (**individual retirement account**) at a brokerage, mutual fund company, or bank.

- You avoid immediate taxes and penalties.
- Your money continues to grow tax-deferred.
- You gain access to wider investment choices than your old employer may have offered.

It's important to understand that a **traditional IRA** lets you save for retirement and may lower your taxable income today since contributions can be tax deductible. Your investments grow without being taxed yearly, but you will pay taxes when you take the money out later.

A **Roth IRA** is a little different—you pay taxes on the money before you put it in, but once it's in the account, the money grows tax-free, and qualified withdrawals during retirement aren't taxed. The biggest difference between a traditional IRA and a Roth IRA is *when* you pay taxes—*now* with a Roth or *later* with a traditional.

Both are different from a 401(k), which is usually offered by an employer, often comes with a company match, and has higher contribution limits. IRAs are opened by individuals, giving you more control over investment choices but without the employer perks.[162]

162 Fernando, "401(k) Plans: What Are They, How They Work."

Important—you must complete the rollover within *sixty days* of withdrawing funds to avoid taxes and penalties. I've taken this step multiple times with success.

Table 8.2 compares key features between a 401(k) and an IRA.

- Contribution limits are much higher for 401(k)s.
- Employer matches are only available with 401(k)s.
- Investment options are broader with an IRA.
- Both have similar tax treatment and withdrawal rules at fifty-nine and a half years.

401(k) Versus IRA Key Feature Comparison

Feature	401(k)	IRA
Contribution Limit (2024)	Up to $23,000 per year (higher if age 50+)	Up to $7,000 per year (higher if age 50+)
Employer Match	Often available depending on employer plan	Not available
Investment Options	Limited to employer plan options	Broader choices such as stocks, ETFs, mutual funds, and bonds
Tax Treatment	Traditional (tax-deferred) or Roth	Traditional or Roth depending on eligibility

Note: Contribution limits shown are for 2024. Employer matching is generally only in employer-sponsored 401(k) plans. Both accounts may offer Traditional (tax-deferred) or Roth tax treatment depending on eligibility.

Table 8.2 Source: Your Blueprint for Financial Literacy

Leave it with your former employer. Some companies allow you to leave your 401(k) in the old plan indefinitely—usually if your balance is $5,000 or more. However, you can no longer contribute. This might make sense if the plan is well managed and offers strong investment options. But be cautious: Over time, people can lose track of old retirement accounts, especially after changing jobs multiple times. In my case, I left funds in a retirement account overseas because moving it to a US-based account would have triggered heavy fees. But unless you're in a similar situation, I wouldn't recommend this path.

Transfer it to your new employer's plan. Another smart option is to roll your old 401(k) into your new employer's plan. This keeps your retirement funds in one place, and you avoid taxes and penalties. Plus, your new plan's administrator often helps guide the process. If you prefer not to manage an IRA on your own, this is a simple and effective way to maintain tax-deferred growth.

Is It Ever a Good Idea to Take Early Withdrawals?

In most cases, no. as mentioned earlier, withdrawing from your 401(k) before age fifty-nine and a half means paying a 10% penalty, plus income tax. However, some employers do allow **hardship withdrawals** for emergencies, like medical bills, funeral expenses, or down payments on a home. These situations may allow you to avoid the penalty—but you'll still owe taxes.[163]

There are some differences internationally. For example, in the UK, some private pensions or retirement plans allow individuals age fifty-five or over to withdraw up to 25% tax-free.

As mentioned earlier, I also have a retirement fund in the UK. Unfortunately, those same rules don't apply here in the US. Unless absolutely necessary, I would avoid touching your retirement savings early. The long-term impact can be significant—and the lost growth over time is difficult to recover.

What's a Stock Market?

We just covered retirement—but one of the most important tools to

163 Fernando, "401(k) Plans: What Are They, How They Work."

help fund it is the **stock market**. The stock market isn't a single physical place but rather a system where shares of publicly traded companies are bought and sold, mostly online.[164] The market plays two major roles: It allows companies to raise money by offering shares of ownership, and it serves as a gauge of the economy's overall health.

When I opened my Roth IRA, which wasn't offered through an employer, I had to learn more about how the stock market works. Investing is not just for the wealthy—anyone can get involved, whether they're saving for retirement, building wealth, or hoping to grow their money over time. People invest in stocks for different reasons:

- Some are after **dividends**, a share of company profits.
- Others try to buy low and sell high.
- Some investors value the **voting rights** they get with ownership.

Stock prices fluctuate based on supply and demand, company performance, economic trends, and even investor emotions. That unpredictability—known as **market sentiment**—makes research essential.

How the Stock Market Works

The stock market is a regulated environment that allows investors to buy and sell shares. It connects those who need capital (businesses) with those who want to invest (individuals or institutions).[165]

Not every business can sell stocks to the public. To do so, a company must go through an **initial public offering (IPO)**. After that, their shares can be traded on major stock exchanges like the **New York Stock Exchange (NYSE)** or **NASDAQ**. IPOs are how major companies like Amazon, Tesla, and Microsoft first entered

164 Peter Gratton, "What Is the Stock Market and How Does It Work?," Investopedia, May 14, 2025, https://www.investopedia.com/terms/s/stockmarket.asp.

165 Gratton, "What Is the Stock Market and How Does It Work?"

the public market. But just because a company has a flashy IPO doesn't mean it will succeed.

I learned this firsthand. I once invested $6,000 in Rivian, an electric vehicle company, when its stock debuted at around $104 per share. At the time of writing this book, the price had dropped to around $10 per share. Will it bounce back? Maybe. Maybe not. The lesson? Do your homework. Don't buy stock just because it's hyped. Study the company's products, outlook, and long-term demand.

What Are Stocks?

When you buy a stock (also called a **share**), you're buying a small portion of a company. The number of shares you own, compared to the total shares available, determines how much ownership you have. Larger companies often issue millions or billions of shares. Owning stock gives you the right to **profit sharing** (**dividends**) and sometimes the right to vote on corporate matters.[166]

What's a Stock Exchange?

Once a company goes public, its shares are traded on a **stock exchange**, which is part of the broader stock market. Major US exchanges include the NYSE and NASDAQ. There are also international exchanges, like the London, Tokyo, and Shanghai stock exchanges.

These exchanges offer three key benefits that help both companies and investors:[167]

- Liquidity, the ability to buy or sell quickly
- Transparency, the ability to see prices in real time
- Investor confidence, built through rules that promote fair trading

166 Gratton, "What Is the Stock Market and How Does It Work?"

167 Gratton, "What Is the Stock Market and How Does It Work?"

Companies may even **cross-list** on multiple exchanges to attract more investors, meaning companies list their stock on more than one exchange to reach more investors and boost their stock's visibility and trading.

The stock market and pop culture. If you're new to investing and want a humorous look at how chaotic the market can be, check out the movie *Trading Places*, starring Eddie Murphy. It's a funny introduction to commodities trading and Wall Street antics. For a more modern (and wild) portrayal, try *The Wolf of Wall Street*, starring Leonardo DiCaprio. It's entertaining—but not a model for how to handle your investments. Every time I think about investing, a classic saying comes to mind: You need to know when to stay invested, when to cut your losses, when to step back and reassess your strategy, and when to exit completely to protect your finances. That advice applies just as much to the stock market as it does to life.

What's a Mutual Fund?

Mutual funds pool money from many investors to purchase a diversified portfolio of stocks, bonds, or other securities. These funds are managed by professional fund managers who make investment decisions based on the fund's stated goals, as outlined in its **prospectus**. That's a document that explains what an investment is, how it works, and what risks are involved—like a brochure that tells you what you're getting into before you invest. When you buy shares of a mutual fund, you become a partial owner of all the assets held in that fund.[168]

The fund's performance—and the value of your shares—depends on how well the underlying investments perform. If the portfolio increases in value, your shares grow in worth. If it declines, your shares lose value. Mutual funds play a large role in retirement investing, especially for middle-income people in the US. In fact, your 401(k) likely includes one or more mutual funds. About half

168 Adam Hayes, "Investing in Mutual Funds: What They Are and How They Work," Investopedia, January 30, 2025, https://www.investopedia.com/terms/m/mutualfund.asp.

of all mutual fund holdings by US households are in **index equity funds**, which aim to mirror the performance of major indexes like the S&P 500 or the Dow Jones Industrial Average.[169]

Common Categories of Mutual Funds

Understanding the various types of mutual funds is important, especially if you're planning for retirement. Here are some common categories of mutual funds:[170]

Stock funds. These funds primarily invest in **equities** (stocks) that break down into subcategories:

- By company size. Small-cap, mid-cap, and large-cap refer to how big the company is.
    - **Small-cap** are smaller companies that are still growing.
    - **Mid-cap** are medium-sized companies that are more stable but still growing.
    - **Large-cap** are big, well-known companies.
- By strategy. Growth, income, or value-oriented refer to what the investment is trying to do.
    - **Growth** means investing in companies expected to grow fast.
    - **Income** means investing in companies that pay you money (dividends).
    - **Value-oriented** means investing in companies that are a good deal (cheap for what they're worth).
- By geography. Domestic (US) or international refers to where the company is from.

169 Gratton, "What Is the Stock Market and How Does It Work?"

170 Gratton, "What Is the Stock Market and How Does It Work?"

- **Domestic** means companies are from the US.
- **International** means companies are from other countries.

Bond funds. Bond funds fall under the fixed-income category. They invest in debt securities like these:

- **Government bonds** are loans you give to the government, and they pay you back later with interest.
- **Corporate bonds** are loans you give to a company, and they promise to pay you back with interest.
- **Municipal bonds** or other debt instruments are loans to cities, states, or other groups; they also pay you back with interest, often with tax breaks.

These funds aim to provide steady interest income, which is distributed to shareholders. Risk levels vary based on the type of bonds held; high-yield or "junk" bond funds, for example, carry much more risk than funds holding US Treasury bonds.

Index mutual funds. Designed to replicate the performance of specific indexes (like the S&P 500), **index mutual funds** are known for three characteristics:

- Lower fees. Index mutual funds cost less because no one is actively picking stocks; the fund just follows the market through passive management.
- Broad market exposure. You own a little piece of lots of different companies, not just a few.
- Consistently strong long-term returns. Over many years, index mutual funds usually grow your money steadily, even if the fund goes up and down in the short term.

Index mutual funds are a popular choice for cost-conscious investors and often outperform actively managed funds over time.

Income funds. These funds aim to provide regular income and are often favored by retirees. **Income funds** invest in two types of loans:

- **High-quality corporate bonds** are loans to big, trusted companies that are more likely to pay you back with steady interest.
- **Government debt**, like a US Treasury bond, is a loan to the government. These loans are seen as very safe because the government usually pays its debts.

The goal is not capital appreciation but steady cash flow through interest payments.

International mutual funds. These funds invest in foreign markets only. A similar type, **global funds**, invests across both domestic and international markets. **International mutual funds** add diversification to a portfolio. They help you spread your money around so you're not putting all your eggs in one basket. They also may reduce overall portfolio risk by balancing domestic downturns. If the US market drops, investments in other countries might not drop as much, helping to balance things out. However, global funds come with additional risk due to currency fluctuation and foreign market volatility. Since money values and markets in other countries can change a lot, these investments can be riskier.

Socially responsible mutual funds. Also known as **SRIs**, these funds follow ethical investing criteria, excluding companies that operate in industries like tobacco, alcohol, weapons, or nuclear energy. Others focus on sustainability, prioritizing companies in renewable energy or those with strong environmental, social, and governance practices. **Socially responsible mutual funds** allow investors to align their investments with their personal values.

Mutual funds offer a convenient way to diversify your portfolio, especially when you're just starting out or building a retirement account. Whether you're looking for long-term growth, income, or socially conscious investing, there's likely a fund that fits your goals.

Will Investing Ensure My Future Retirement?

There are no guarantees in life—and that certainly applies to investing. No one can promise you what your investments will be worth in the future. However, making informed decisions and staying engaged in the markets you've invested in can go a long way toward helping secure your financial future. Contributing to a 401(k) or investing in the stock market are common and effective strategies, but they're not the only ways to build wealth. One phrase you'll often hear in the financial world is *diversifying your investment portfolio.* Many people assume this only means owning a mix of stocks, bonds, and mutual funds—but diversification can go far beyond that.

The most important investment is *you*! One of the greatest investments you can make is in yourself. That means continually working on your education, maintaining your health, and strengthening your mental and emotional well-being. Investing in yourself can increase your value not only as a professional but also as a parent, partner, or leader. Gaining new skills, certifications, or knowledge can open doors to higher income opportunities and personal growth.

Alternate Forms of Investment

Over the years, I've explored many ways to invest outside the traditional markets, including these options:

- Sports trading cards
- Comic books
- Rental properties

- Art
- Older rare books (pre-1900s)

I once bought a sports card for thirty-five dollars. Years later, it was appraised at around $60,000. That doesn't mean it will hold that value forever, but it's a reminder of the potential in alternate assets. My brother, for example, invests in classic and vintage cars. Others buy land, hoping it appreciates over time. These are all examples of portfolio diversification. Whether your investments are traditional or unconventional, the goal remains the same: to place your money in areas where it has the potential to grow in value. The more thoughtful and well-rounded your approach, the stronger your financial foundation can become.

Before we conclude, I want to leave you with a word of caution. A dear friend of mine, Yasir Mansour, who lives in London, once shared a piece of advice that stayed with me: "Remember, you can make money through investing, but you can also lose money. Therefore, never invest more than you can afford to lose—because you can lose it."

CHAPTER 8 KEY TAKEAWAYS

You should now have a better understanding of the following:

- ✓ **Retirement planning basics.** Understanding why saving for retirement matters—and knowing what options are out there—can help you choose the right way to save and invest for your future.
- ✓ **Investment insight.** Understanding retirement plans like 401(k)s and different investment vehicles will empower you to take control of your financial future.
- ✓ **Long-term security.** Knowledge about investing strategies will help you make informed decisions to ensure a comfortable retirement.

Source: Your Blueprint for Financial Literacy

Chapter 9

Dealing with Layoffs and Unemployment

The information in this chapter affects people in the workforce daily. I lived in Japan and one thing I remember, probably more than anything else from that time, except the word *mizu*, which means *water*, is that the Japanese people take pride in working for one company their entire career.

I thought it was very impressive. One of their mottos in Japan is "Quality is job won." Another motto is "We take the best from around the world and make it our own." In those days, any electronic items or cars made in Japan were considered to be top value for your money. Japan had a very stable economy. I never saw a person begging on the streets the entire two years I lived there. Every person took pride in their jobs: the CEOs, the train drivers, the florists, the bathroom cleaners, the street cleaners. It was amazing to see such pride in one's work.

While I write this chapter, my nephew, Samuel, we call him Apple, and several of his friends are visiting Japan for the first time. As I reflect, here in the United States, the conditions were and are totally different, especially in today's job market. Being laid off is one thing; being fired is a whole other demon. Most people never expect it to happen, and very few are ready when it does. You can lose your job in several ways: being laid off, getting fired, resigning, or the company going out of business. I've gone through all of these situations, with the exception of being fired.

I read an article some months ago on Indeed.com that said that it's not good to work for one company too long. The reason is you can miss out on money and other opportunities.[171] This is contrary to what I'd learned in the Japanese workforce, but in US society, I agree. During my career, I've worked for several companies. I've gotten laid off from one job only to get a $40,000 pay increase on my next job based on my experience and the demands of the job. If I hadn't been laid off, I'd have missed out on an extra $40,000 per year.

One of the most commonly used phrases you will hear in the workforce by employees is *I need my job.* That statement has held many people hostage in the workplace. I've found out that you don't need your job; you need food, clothing, and shelter. And some (like Dr. Frasier Crane, a TV show character) would say you need work and love. Case in point, no matter how you lose your job, be it the ones mentioned earlier or any other way, you'll still have the same financial obligations. So, the question would be *Is it the job that holds you hostage, or is it really your responsibilities?*

Just as you must save for retirement, you must also save for your present responsibilities, such as utility bills, mortgage payments, car payments, insurance, credit cards, etc. Now, let's add a few we haven't spoken about: children and dependents who rely on you, food, and clothing for different weather. Those are the responsibilities that really hold you hostage if you aren't prepared. Regardless of how you may lose your job, those are the things that you worry about. The job becomes an afterthought. That's when investing in yourself and for the present, not just your retirement, comes into play.

It's widely believed that three to six months of living expenses are what is needed when someone loses their job. Well, that

171 Indeed Editorial Team, "Pros and Cons of Staying for a Long Time with One Employer," updated December 11, 2025, https://www.indeed.com/career-advice/starting-new-job/staying-long-with-one-employer-pros-cons.

depends strongly on your debt-to-savings ratio, how much you have in savings compared to your monthly outgoings at the time you lose your job. My experience has shown me that one year is a good target to have in reserves, and that's being conservative. For many people—including myself—finding a new job during the pandemic took a year or more. Even without a pandemic, that amount of time is possible during your job search. You can't control if you'll lose your job, but you can control how losing a job affects you and your family by investing and saving early. This book was written to point out these important matters in advance. Regardless of your stage in life, this book can be beneficial.

It's been said that you can have too much in savings. Well, ask a person who makes thousands of dollars a year in passive income on their high-interest savings account. Before they answer, you'll probably have to wait a while—until they stop laughing. You can never save too much. If you reach the maximum savings in your account that is protected by the FDIC, open another bank account.

I've been told by investment advisors looking to get my business that inflation can affect the value of money in savings over the years. That's true, but at least you know the money will be there regardless of how the economy or the stock market performs. Saving is what saved me.

Now, on to some serious questions and answers.

Q&A SESSION

What's the Difference Between Being Furloughed and Laid Off?

Investopedia explains the key differences well. Both furloughs and layoffs involve not receiving a paycheck—but the main distinction is that **furloughs** are temporary, while **layoffs** are typically permanent.[172] I, like many others, agree with this distinction. Here are some common signs that you're being furloughed rather than laid off:[173]

- Your employer asks you to stop working for a set period—say, a month—because a major contract is delayed.
- You're asked to take one unpaid week off per quarter due to a projected yearlong slowdown.
- You're given Fridays off until further notice to reduce costs, but you're still employed.
- You're told to use all your paid time off before the end of the year—your hours or pay haven't been cut, but it's a cost-saving measure.

Key Considerations During a Furlough

Maintaining income. See if your employer allows you to use paid time off to offset lost wages. If so, you may lose future time off, but it could help maintain cash flow. Freelance, gig, or contractor work may be an option, but make sure your employer permits it. Some prohibit side work, especially for competitors.

Taxes. Independent work means you'll be responsible for self-employment taxes. That includes quarterly payments. As mentioned earlier, consult a financial adviser if you're unsure about your tax obligations.

Retirement contributions. You might not be able to contribute to a workplace plan during a furlough. However, you can still use an IRA for retirement savings, and you can make your contributions closer to tax time, if needed, to help with cash flow.

172 Amy Fontinelle, "Furlough vs. Layoff," Investopedia, October 22, 2024, https://www.investopedia.com/furlough-vs-layoff-5213743.

173 Fontinelle, "Furlough vs. Layoff."

Back pay. Some furloughed workers—especially federal employees—may receive back pay once the furlough ends, as outlined in the Government Employee Fair Treatment Act of 2019.[174]

What Happens When You're Laid Off?

A layoff means the job is gone—and so are your wages and benefits. You'll need to start job hunting right away. Remember, a layoff is *not* a firing. You've done nothing wrong; your position has simply been eliminated due to budget cuts, restructuring, or lack of work. Layoffs may be temporary, and you may be rehired later if you work in seasonal industries like these:[175]

- Tourism
- Hospitality
- Retail
- Agriculture
- Fishing and hunting

What to Do If You're Laid Off[176]

1. Apply for unemployment benefits. File right away. You paid taxes into the system—now it's your turn to use it.
2. Look into available support. Depending on your income, you may qualify for tax credits or assistance programs:
   - Child Tax Credit
   - Saver's Credit

174 Fontinelle, "Furlough vs. Layoff."
175 Fontinelle, "Furlough vs. Layoff."
176 Fontinelle, "Furlough vs. Layoff."

- Health insurance subsidies
- Food assistance and utility relief
- Student loan forbearance or repayment plans

When I left the US for London, I didn't have a job. I called my educational loan provider and was relieved to hear "Don't worry—we can defer it up to a year." That kind gesture allowed me time to get back on my feet, and I repaid the loan in full once employed.

Key Points to Remember About Layoffs[177]

Severance and taxes. If you qualify for **severance pay**, it can soften the financial blow—but it may also delay unemployment benefits. Both severance and unemployment income must be reported on your tax return. If you're laid off early in the year, your income may be low enough that your overall tax burden is minimal. But if you earned a lot or are quickly rehired, consider adjusting your Form W-4 to withhold more taxes from your next paycheck.

Retirement accounts. Once laid off, you can no longer contribute to an employer plan or receive matching. You may want to open or contribute to a traditional or Roth IRA, depending on your situation. If you have an outstanding loan from your retirement plan, you may need to repay it quickly to avoid taxes and penalties. You'll also need to decide whether to leave your 401(k) with your former employer or roll it over into an IRA.

What Are Your Legal Rights?

To protect workers after furloughs or layoffs, the US has laws and contracts in place, stated in the US Department of Health and Human Services, including these listed:[178]

177 Fontinelle, "Furlough vs. Layoff."

178 Fontinelle, "Furlough vs. Layoff."

- The **Fair Labor Standards Act** sets the rules for minimum wage, overtime pay, and child labor.
- The **Affordable Care Act** helps more people get health insurance and sets rules for how insurance works.
- The **Worker Adjustment and Retraining Act** (federal and state versions) says big companies must give workers a heads-up (usually sixty days) before mass layoffs or closures.
- State unemployment laws help workers get temporary money (unemployment benefits) if they lose their jobs without it being their fault.
- The **Family and Medical Leave Act** lets workers take unpaid time off for big life events, like having a baby or serious illness, without losing their job.
- Union collective bargaining agreements are deals made between worker unions and employers that set rules for pay, benefits, and working conditions.
- Equal employment opportunity laws make sure people can't be treated unfairly at work because of things like their race, gender, age, or religion.

Can You Get Unemployment While Furloughed?

It's possible, receiving unemployment benefits depends on your state's laws and how your employer defines the furlough. If you're still receiving partial pay or benefits, your unemployment eligibility may be limited or reduced. Check with your state unemployment office.[179]

What About Health Insurance?

If you're furloughed, your employer might continue providing

179 Fontinelle, "Furlough vs. Layoff."

benefits. If you're laid off, your severance package may include health insurance for a time. Otherwise, you'll be eligible for **COBRA**, which allows you to keep your employer coverage at your own cost. Alternatively, you can shop for an ACA plan at Healthcare.gov —layoffs qualify you for special enrollment.[180]

Why You Must Save for the Present, Not Just Retirement

Even with access to benefits and programs, they may not cover everything—and they take time to kick in. That's why emergency savings, low debt, and high-yield savings accounts are so important. I've been laid off before and was able to cover utility bills and car payments from the interest alone in my high-yield savings account. That's not just preparation—it's peace of mind.

What Are Unemployment Benefits, and How Do I Apply?

One of the first things people think about after being laid off or furloughed is how to keep money coming in. I once had a friend who refused to apply for unemployment because he felt embarrassed. I've noticed that feeling is common among people who were either proud of their job titles or good salaries. It reminded me of an episode of the old TV show *Good Times*. The family needed to borrow money from a wealthier cousin, only to find out the cousin had been laid off himself. He was too ashamed to tell anyone—even his wife. He would dress up each morning and leave the house in a suit, but he would go to the movies and just walk around the city instead of going to work. Now, my friend Denver has a catchphrase. Any time something goes wrong, he says, "Good times." It wasn't until writing this section that I finally caught the reference—and yes, I literally laughed out loud.

But let's get serious for a moment. If you're eligible for unemployment insurance, you should never feel embarrassed to use it. According to the US Department of Labor's Unemployment Insurance Program, **unemployment benefits**, also known as

180 Fontinelle, "Furlough vs. Layoff."

unemployment insurance, are temporary payments provided to people who've lost their jobs through no fault of their own—like being laid off or furloughed.[181] These benefits are designed to help individuals cover basic living expenses while they actively search for new work. The system is managed at the state level but follows federal guidelines. To be eligible, you typically must meet these conditions:

- You've earned a minimum amount of wages during a defined base period.
- You're actively seeking employment.
- You're available and ready to work.
- You've become unemployed through no fault of your own.

The funding for unemployment benefits comes from taxes paid by employers—not by employees. However, it's important to know that these benefits are considered taxable income and must be reported on your federal tax return.

How to Apply for Unemployment Benefits

Here are the general steps to apply for unemployment benefits, based on US Department of Labor guidance:[182]

1. File a claim in the state where you worked. Visit your state's unemployment insurance website or contact their office by phone to begin your application. If you live in a different state than where you worked, file in the state where the job was located.

181 U.S. Department of Labor, "State Unemployment Insurance Benefits," Employment & Training Administration, accessed August 27, 2025, https://oui.doleta.gov/unemploy/uifactsheet.asp.

182 U.S. Department of Labor, "State Unemployment Insurance Benefits."

2. Prepare your information. You'll typically need your Social Security number, details of your most recent employer (company name, address, phone number), the dates you worked, your total earnings, and the reason for your job separation.
3. Submit the application. File your claim online or by phone, depending on your state's process. It usually takes two to three weeks for the initial claim to be processed.
4. File ongoing weekly or biweekly claims. Once approved, you must continue submitting weekly or biweekly updates confirming you are still unemployed and looking for work. You must also report any income you earn during this time.
5. Stay compliant. Some states may require job search logs, attendance at career workshops, or participation in job-placement programs.

Different Types of Unemployment

There are four major types of unemployment:[183]

- **Cyclical unemployment** is linked to economic downturns (e.g., recessions).
- **Frictional unemployment** occurs when people leave one job to look for another.
- **Institutional unemployment** is caused by laws or policies, such as minimum wage laws.
- **Structural unemployment** is long-term job loss due to economic changes like automation.

183 Julia Kagan, "Unemployment Insurance (UI): How It Works, Requirements, and Funding," Investopedia, July 8, 2024, https://www.investopedia.com/terms/u/unemployment-insurance.asp.

Other Important Notes on Unemployment

- Unemployment benefits are temporary. Most states offer benefits up to twenty-six weeks, with potential extensions depending on economic conditions.[184]
- Unemployment benefits are taxable. Make sure you choose to have taxes withheld, or you could owe money come tax season.
- If you're doing freelance work or you're paid in cash while claiming unemployment, you must report it.
- Treat unemployment benefits as a bridge, not a permanent solution. Combine them with emergency savings if possible.

Unemployment benefits can make a huge difference during tough times, but they won't replace your full paycheck—and they aren't forever. This is why saving while you're working is critical.

And remember, there's no shame in needing help. If you're eligible, use it.

What's the Difference Between Being a Contractor and a Full-Time Employee?

I've been both a **full-time employee** and a **contractor**, and both come with their own set of advantages and challenges. In general, a full-time employee works a set number of hours—typically around thirty hours per week or 120 hours per month—in exchange for a regular salary or hourly wage. These positions tend to offer financial stability, benefits, and paid time off, but they often come with less control over when and how you work.[185]

Let's explore the pros and cons of full-time employment:[186]

184 Kagan, "Unemployment Insurance (UI): How It Works, Requirements, and Funding."

185 Upwork Team, "Contract vs. Full-Time Employment: Key Differences Explained," Upwork Resource Center, August 27, 2024, https://www.upwork.com/resources/full-time-job-vs-contract-work.

186 Upwork Team, "Contract vs. Full-Time Employment: Key Differences Explained."

Advantages of Full-Time Employment

- Job security. There's consistent work week to week, with less worry about constantly seeking new projects.
- Benefits. Employees have access to health insurance, life insurance, and retirement plans.
- Social Security support. You only pay half of your Social Security and Medicare taxes—your employer covers the rest.
- Short-term disability coverage. Paid leave options are available if you face a medical emergency or crisis.
- Paid time off. Vacation days, holidays, and sick leave are typically part of the package.
- Growth opportunities. Employees have paths to promotions, leadership roles, and internal job mobility.
- Fixed schedule. Generally, employees have set or consistent hours or shifts, making planning easier.
- Company perks. Depending on company culture, you may enjoy social events, wellness programs, or gym memberships.
- Financial consistency. Predictable income makes it easier to plan and manage monthly expenses.
- Training and development. Many employers offer workshops, classes, or skill development programs.

Disadvantages of Full-Time Employment

- Routine burnout. The repetition of daily tasks can become dull over time.

- Limited resume. Staying too long in one role may limit your skill set. I've countered this by earning certifications and taking professional development courses throughout my career.
- Work stress. Long hours or repetitive tasks can lead to fatigue or anxiety outside of work.
- Limited autonomy. You may have less control over your schedule or location than a contractor would.

What Is Contract Work?

Contract workers are hired to complete specific tasks for a set period of time. They are similar to freelancers and are usually paid a rate or project fee instead of a salary. Many contract workers serve multiple clients at once and often have specialized expertise that allows them to negotiate higher pay. However, they are typically not eligible for employee benefits, and work can be inconsistent.[187]

Advantages of Contract Work

- Growing demand. A 2022 McKinsey American Opportunity Survey showed that 36% of US workers are contract-based—up significantly from just a few years ago.[188]
- Flexible schedule. Contractors can often choose their working hours as long as deadlines are met.
- Control over projects. You can accept or decline assignments based on their alignment with your interests or expertise.
- Higher earning potential. Contractors may charge more than salaried workers—especially in specialized fields.

187 Upwork Team, "Contract vs. Full-Time Employment: Key Differences Explained."

188 Upwork Team, "Contract vs. Full-Time Employment: Key Differences Explained."

Disadvantages of Contract Work

- Job uncertainty. Contracts can end abruptly, and securing new clients can be unpredictable.
- Lack of benefits. Contract workers are not eligible for employer-sponsored health insurance, paid time off, or retirement matches.
- No paid leave. If you don't work, you don't get paid—so vacations come at a cost.
- Self-employment taxes. Contractors are responsible for paying the full 15.3% FICA tax (Social Security and Medicare).
- Out-of-pocket business expenses. You pay for your own software, supplies, travel, and equipment, but you may deduct eligible costs when filing taxes.

In my experience, both work arrangements can be rewarding—if you understand what you're signing up for. Full-time jobs offer structure and stability, while contract work offers freedom and flexibility, often with higher income potential but also higher risk. In the next section, we'll explore how your wages and taxes differ between these types of positions and why understanding this could make a big difference in your financial planning.

What's the Difference Between a W-2 and a 1099?

Yes, you guessed right. I've worked as both a W-2 employee and a 1099 independent contractor, and I can say each has its own advantages. From my experience, being a 1099 worker gave me greater control over my time and allowed for more tax deductions.

According to QuickBooks, understanding the difference between these two classifications is essential—especially when it comes to tax season.[189]

What Is a 1099 Worker?

The **1099 form** is used to report income paid to individuals who are not traditional employees. These are the two most common types of 1099s for contract workers:[190]

- **1099-NECs** are used to report payments of $600 or more for nonemployee compensation.
- **1099-MISCs** are used for other types of miscellaneous income.

These forms are typically issued to freelancers, gig workers, and independent contractors. Businesses hire 1099 workers for specific tasks or projects, and unlike employees, they don't receive benefits or have taxes withheld from their pay. If you're classified as a 1099 worker, you're considered self-employed, which means you're responsible for paying your own income taxes, Social Security, and Medicare taxes, as mentioned earlier. You're also in charge of providing your own equipment, software, or tools to do the job.

What Is a W-2 Worker?

By contrast, **W-2 employees** work directly for a company—either full-time or part-time—and receive a regular paycheck. At the end of each calendar year, employers issue **Form W-2**, which provides details about your annual income, contributions, and withholdings among other things.[191]

189 Ana Bentes, "1099 vs W-2: What's the Difference in 2026?" QuickBooks Payroll, November 25, 2025, https://quickbooks.intuit.com/payroll/1099-vs-w2/.

190 Bentes, "1099 vs W-2: What's the Difference in 2026?"

191 Bentes, "1099 vs W-2: What's the Difference in 2026?"

- Taxable income is your total earnings and how much was withheld for federal taxes.
- FICA contributions are your withholdings for Social Security and Medicare.
- State taxes are the amount withheld for your state's income tax.
- Social Security tax withheld
- Medicare tax withheld
- Dependent care benefits
- Retirement contributions
- Health insurance contributions

As a W-2 employee, you're eligible for employee benefits like health insurance, paid time off, overtime pay, and employer-sponsored retirement plans. As stated earlier, the employer is responsible for paying half of your FICA taxes and must provide necessary tools or supplies. This classification offers more structure and legal protection and is the default classification for workers who don't meet the criteria for independent contracting.

W-2 Versus 1099: My Perspective

While a W-2 job comes with important protections and steady benefits, I've found that with the right skills and network, a 1099 worker can often earn more and build greater financial independence over time. As a contractor, I appreciated the ability to deduct business expenses—something W-2 employees can't typically do unless they meet specific IRS criteria. These deductions can include things like these:

- Home office expenses

- Work-related travel
- Equipment and software
- Marketing or advertising costs

Tax filing reminder—when preparing your annual tax return, both the W-2 and 1099 forms are essential. If you've worked both types of jobs in the same year, be sure to collect each document to accurately report your income.

In short, W-2s are issued by your employer and report income that already had taxes withheld. A 1099 reports income with no taxes withheld, which means it's on you to track and report that income properly. Understanding the differences between these two roles can help you make more informed decisions about your career—and how you manage your money.

CHAPTER 9 KEY TAKEAWAYS

You should now have a better understanding of the following:

- ✓ **Employment terminology.** Knowing the difference between things like furloughs, layoffs, and employment status can help you better understand and manage the ups and downs of your career.
- ✓ **Unemployment resources.** Information on unemployment benefits and application processes will guide you in effectively managing job loss.
- ✓ **Tax implications.** Understanding the differences between W-2 and 1099 forms will prepare you for the complexities of tax reporting in different employment situations.

Source: Your Blueprint for Financial Literacy

Chapter 10

Financial Lessons from Travel and Real-World Experience

The Six P's to Success

I learned about the six P's to success from a New York University professor named Ed Able. Ed was one of the best professors I've ever had. His teaching took away lots of fear when it came to understanding business ownership. He advised us that, to be successful in whatever we do, we'd need to always make sure we have the six P's present in our efforts.[192]

- We must have *patience*. Nothing will happen simply because we really want it to happen.
- We must have a *plan*, not just an idea. An idea without planning and action will get no bigger than the brain cell it took to think of the idea.
- We must be *persistent*. When things don't go our way, we must remember that ease is a bigger threat to success than hardship. If you get knocked down seven times, get back up eight.
- We must *practice*. The great Stephen Curry, of the Golden State Warriors, didn't come out and start

192 Ed Able. "6 P's Are the Keys to Success." Jim Blasingame: The Small Business Advocate, March 7, 2012, https://m.smallbusinessadvocate.com/small-business-article/6-ps-are-the-keys-to-success-2629.

making three pointers just because he is a product of another great three-point shooter, his dad. Stephen had to practice and practice, and when he was tired, he had to practice.

- We must have *passion* for what we are trying to achieve. I used to listen to street musicians, and one of the things some of them lacked was passion. They were simply playing for the money from tourists' donations or maybe for someone to feel sorry for them. When they performed with passion, I could hear their soul, hence the term *soul music.*
- To succeed, we must keep a *positive attitude.* A negative attitude will only make us focus on the worst thoughts and will surely get in the way of progress. No matter how hard the setback, always keep a positive attitude.

How to Create SMART Goals

Having goals in life is good, and using a **SMART goal** road map can make your goals a lot easier to achieve. Being organized is very important. The acronym *SMART* stands for specific, measurable, achievable, relevant, and time-bound. SMART goals are usually aligned with business; however, you can use them for your personal goals as well. These five characteristics are important to remember when reaching for your goal, be it getting your university or college degree or saving money to become financially secure.

Indeed gives clear examples of how to set up SMART goals, based on the model originally popularized by George T. Doran.[193] I've paraphrased them a bit here to apply to individuals instead of businesses.

Specific. Defining your goals precisely increases your chances of accomplishing them. Set very specific, highly detailed goals

193 Indeed Employer Content Team. "SMART Goals: An Acronym for Success." Indeed, last updated July 15, 2025, https://www.indeed. com/hire/c/info/smart-goals.

because goals are simpler to reach when they're crystal clear. To do this, remove ambiguity from the process by asking a few questions. By laying out what you expect from the outset, you will know what success looks like. Additionally, setting and refining specific goals helps you direct your actions and thoughts toward a common purpose.

Measurable. Data and metrics fuel successful life tasks, and tracking progress toward your goal with numbers helps keep you laser focused. To make your goals measurable, develop metrics that show you bird's-eye views of important information, then detail the key performance indicators that help quantify advancements. I use a Microsoft Excel spreadsheet to help me determine what's in progress and what needs to be completed for my life goals. This was very useful when selling an investment property. You always must measure progress to see if you're on track to reach your goals.

Achievable. By creating goals that are achievable and attainable, you increase your chances of success. Achievable goals rely on specificity and measurability, as well as realism. When you understand that you can meet your goal due to good planning and tracking, you'll have more confidence going forward. Part of setting achievable goals is keeping yourself motivated and following the blueprint you've created to guide your progress.

Relevant. In this context, *relevant* means aligning your goals with the broader objectives of what you're trying to achieve. By focusing on what's truly important, you're more likely to effectively advance your ambitions. Relevancy in your SMART goals offers a compass that points the way toward success.

Time-bound. By making goals time-bound, you prevent procrastination. Framing goals as time-bound provides a sense of urgency and the opportunity to schedule the steps toward your ambitions. During your assessment, consider which objectives lay the foundation for your goals and which must come later in the process. I have a friend named Lauryn who is working on becoming an ob-gyn, and she was in a rush to get there. By not properly evaluating what was attainable within the time she allotted to achieve her goals, she became burned out and had to take a semester off to regroup. Remember—you haven't failed unless you give up. You just have some obstacles you must overcome. Lauryn understood that and got back on track.

You May Want More Than You Need

I used to look at magazines with my great-great-grandmother as a child. I was amazed by the people and places in the pictures I saw, especially in *Life Magazine*. It was full of foreign places and cultures that were intriguing to me as a child. I knew from an early age that I'd travel to see these places and that I'd marry someone who was from a totally different background and environment to me. Living in the US gave me the urge to possess everything in great portions: a large house, a big car, plenty of food, and lots of clothes. But as I traveled the world, I realized the importance of understanding what you *want* compared to what you *need* in life.

Seeing poverty in both developed and developing countries helped me to realize the importance of moderation and not excess. I remember hearing about an athlete who bought five or six cars of the same make and model but the colors were different. I think he later came to a rational decision that it was a mistake and thought about other things he could have used that money for. Sometimes, more is just more and not actually better. I invite you to travel and experience poverty, not just in other countries but in your own cities and states. You'll see clearly that you sometimes want more than you need.

Important Things to Remember About Investing

Back in 2015, I used to really worry about my retirement. Although I was working, I didn't have a 401(k). My company didn't offer one. My private pension in London was unobtainable, and I couldn't transfer it to a retirement account here. I decided to do something about my worries and opened a Roth IRA with Fidelity after reading about investing. I needed $2,500 to start. Without it, I could open an account, but I couldn't start to trade until I reached that number.

With the aid of an account advisor at Fidelity, the first mutual fund I bought was GTLOX, which stands for Glenmede Disciplined US Equity Portfolio. From there, I went on to learn more about some of the things I spoke about in this book, and my investment portfolio is much more diverse now. I learned to watch the markets on the business channels, only to discover that they pretty much say the same thing repeatedly throughout the day unless something major occurs. I also learned that those little numbers crawling on the bottom of the screen on the business channels don't seem to move so quickly when you understand what they mean.

When you pick a stock or mutual fund, my advice is to understand two important things: (1) What are the services the company in the stock or the companies in the mutual funds offer, and (2) are those services and products something that is wanted or needed by the world at large? If so, the products will be in high demand, making the stock or mutual fund more attractive and valuable.

One important initialism to learn in investing is *IPO*, which means initial public offering. IPOs are companies that are about to start trading on the stock market, and they need to raise money. They're willing to sell shares in their company via the stock market. The key is to buy a stock or mutual fund at a low price and hope it increases in value. Stocks like Microsoft and Tesla are impressive, but they're established companies. They could be too high in cost for the average person just starting to trade or purchase stocks. If you consider where those stocks' prices were when they started and their value now, they're truly impressive, but the key, again, is to buy stock and mutual funds at reasonable prices and hope they increase in value.

Understand what the company does before buying their shares. Morningstar is a brilliant site that breaks down any stock or mutual fund you may want to know more about before investing in them. Companies like Fidelity and Vanguard do an excellent job with this as well. Stock Analysis is a great site to get a glimpse of what IPOs are coming to the market or have just launched. You can research any new IPO coming to the market by typing https://stockanalysis.com/ipos/calendar/ in your search browser.

How Saving Money Saved Me

You've read in earlier chapters about the importance of saving. I remember when my wife, Zenaye, and I first moved to New York City from London. I was simply moving back to the US, but she'd only visited the US. Neither of us had ever lived in New York; we'd only visited it on a few occasions while living in London. Neither of us had jobs when we moved, but the one thing we did have was our savings. Our move proved Richard Gere's line from the movie *Pretty Woman*: "Stores are never nice to people; they're nice to credit cards."[194] In my case, it wasn't credit cards, it was money.

We flew to New York on several occasions to look at apartments since we needed to secure something prior to moving here. We had to pay a year's rent in advance to secure the apartment. I remember all the people experiencing homelessness that I saw on the streets, and I realized there's nothing more important when relocating than having a safe place to live and rest at night. The up-front rent assured us that for one entire year, no matter what our work situation, we'd have a place to call home. The rent was our biggest outgoing expense. Once we secured jobs, we were able to save at a much better rate because the biggest cost was taken care of for the entire year. Saving our money saved us from unnecessary headaches.

Cheap Is Expensive

Some people learn this statement, as my friend Safi would say, the hard way. My experience has taught me that, whatever item you purchase, make sure it's an item of good quality if you can afford to do so. Keep in mind, I didn't say to make sure it's expensive. I said *good quality*. We once bought a couch made of faux leather, which

194 Pretty Woman, directed by Garry Marshall (1990; Touchstone Pictures).

is much less durable than real leather. It tends to crack and peel over time, with poor-quality pieces losing their original finish in just a few months. Because faux leather is manmade, this peeling and cracking can't be undone, and the sofa continued to degrade over time. That couch deteriorated within a year. We then purchased a sofa made of real leather, and it's still in great condition ten years later. Some people in society tend to believe that if something is expensive, it's of good quality. I've seen designer bags made of faux leather for sale for hundreds of dollars in retail stores. I've seen where rental property owners have held off on fixing issues in their units only to let things get worse, then pay double or triple the price they'd have paid if they'd taken care of the issue when it was first brought to their attention. Cheap is truly expensive.

Never Be in a Rush to Fail

Remember the home-buying section of this book? This is a subject where many people have set themselves up to fail. These are the real questions: Do you *need* or *want* to buy a home, and can you afford to buy a home at that moment? My niece Summer got married and came to New York as one of her stops on her honeymoon. She and her new spouse had relocated to Atlanta, and they asked what advice I could give them on buying a home. My rule of thumb is that if you decide to make a big purchase, such as a home, make sure you have enough money in reserves in case one or both of you lose your jobs, and that the payments are at a level where one person could cover them if they're still working.

People confuse what it really means to not be able to afford something. It's not that you can't afford it—it's that you can't afford to purchase it at that moment. So, go back and save more money. That way you're able to make a larger down payment, or you can get rid of bills that are unnecessary and cost you high interest payments that prevent you from reaching your target. This could bring the home price into a range that you could afford. At the same time, this strategy will save you thousands of dollars in interest over the finance period of the mortgage by putting down a larger payment or by paying a bit more toward the principal of the loan every month.

There's no need to rush. You don't need to rush to buy a home; what you need is a nice, relaxing, safe place to live that meets your needs at that moment. Remember, you'll have lots of obstacles in life. You want to make sure *you* aren't one of those obstacles getting in your own way.

Time Isn't Usually on Your Side

Few statements are truer than this. I remember sitting in the back seat of Mr. Eddie Mac Turner's station wagon when I was in the Head Start program as a four-year-old. I remember all the kids in my class crying on the first day of school. I remember biting the back of the seat in front of me, where the girls sat, and I chipped my front tooth in that station wagon. I'm much older now, and as I look back on those earlier years, it reminds me of the old saying that time flies. Time is very valuable. Spend your time wisely. Don't waste it. Don't procrastinate when you have ideas or goals. I've found time to be more precious than money or any rare stone. No amount of money can buy back time you've wasted.

One day, an older Greek man who had cancer gave me a poem, "Ithaka." It shows us the true meaning of life and how to wisely spend our time. BookRags study guide states the meaning of Ithaka: "Just as the journey to Ithaka is a metaphor for the human journey through life, so Ithaka is a metaphor for all destinations. It represents all the goals and ideals that humans strive for, all the expectations of a reward to be received in the future for actions performed in the present."[195] I always keep a copy of the poem with me in some form, and I only share it with people who I believe really need it and will understand it.

195 BookRags, "Style in Ithaka." *In Ithaka Study Guide*, accessed August 9, 2025, https://www.bookrags.com/studyguide-ithaka/style.html.

Don't Spend Too Much Time Dreaming

I, like many people, dream a lot. However, I stopped having life dreams. What I mean by this is that I tend to replace what we dream of with life ambitions to accomplish. I've had many dreams while asleep, but I've never awakened to find even one of them to be true. Replace dreams with ambitions backed up with actions and hard work. As stated earlier, an idea with no actions behind it will get no bigger than the brain cell it took to think of the idea. If you fall seven times, get back up eight. Remember, ease in life is a bigger threat to progress than hardship.

It's Not How Much the Other Person Knows When You're Negotiating—It's How Much You Don't Know

I was required to read a book called *The Skilled Negotiator* while in a project management course at New York University's continuous professional studies program. NYU is where I met Ed Able, the professor I mentioned earlier. There were two statements in that book I will always remember:[196]

1. "The Stranger may be found not only across the breakfast table but in the mirror as well."
2. "Setting oneself on a predetermined course into unknown waters is the perfect way to sail straight into an iceberg."

Several subjects that we've covered consist of some sort of negotiating skills needed on your behalf, like buying a home or car or choosing the correct bank account. Having the knowledge from this book will drive you to dig deeper and get an even better understanding when you are making decisions about these matters. You'll be able to make the best choices for you

196 Mary Catherine Bateson, quoted in Kathleen Kelley Reardon, *The Skilled Negotiator: Mastering the Language of Engagement* (San Francisco: Jossey-Bass, 2004), 10.
Henry Mintzberg, quoted in Kathleen Kelley Reardon, The Skilled Negotiator: Mastering the Language of Engagement (San Francisco: Jossey-Bass, 2004), 36

and avoid unnecessary expenses. You can pay hundreds or even thousands of dollars more on the purchase of a house due to a lack of knowledge and negotiating skills. Knowledge is what enables us to negotiate.

I hope you enjoyed our conversations as much as I have during our personal finance journey together. With this information, you'll be able to go forward with more confidence when faced with these financial challenges in life. This information is designed to make those tasks less challenging. And as Aunt Little Bit would say, "Now, ain't that something for your money!"

BIBLIOGRAPHY

The following sources were used for research and fact verification throughout this book. All referenced material has been paraphrased and interpreted in the author's own words, with full credit given to the original publishers for their foundational content.

Able, Ed. "6 P's Are the Keys to Success." Jim Blasingame: The Small Business Advocate. March 7, 2012. https://m.smallbusinessadvocate.com/small-business-article/6-ps-are-the-keys-to-success-2629.

Araj, Victoria. "What's the Difference Between a Mortgage and an Auto Loan?" Quicken Loans. March 8, 2024. https://www.quickenloans.com/learn/whats-the-difference-between-a-mortgage-and-an-auto-loan.

Bank of America. "8 Common Bank Fees—and How to Avoid Them." Better Money Habits by Bank of America. Accessed August 2025. https://bettermoneyhabits.bankofamerica.com/en/personal-banking/avoid-bank-fees.

Bank of America. "Bank of America Preferred Rewards." Accessed July 7, 2025. https://promotions.bankofamerica.com/preferredrewards/en#requirements.

Banton, Caroline. "Interest Rates: Types and What They Mean to Borrowers." Investopedia. May 11, 2025. https://www.investopedia.com/terms/i/interestrate.asp.

Barone, Adam. "How Banking Works, Types of Banks, and How to Choose the Best Bank for You." Investopedia. March 28, 2023. https://www.investopedia.com/terms/b/bank.asp.

Barry, Keith. "How to Test-Drive a New or Used Car." *Consumer Reports*, April 7, 2025. https://www.consumerreports.org/cars/buying-a-car/how-to-test-drive-a-new-or-used-car-a4558551981.

Bentes, Ana. "1099 vs W-2: What's the Difference in 2026?" QuickBooks Payroll. November 25, 2025. https://quickbooks.intuit.com/payroll/1099-vs-w2/.

Black, Michelle L. "Heading to the Car Dealership? Get a Great Deal by Following These 9 Steps." Investopedia. February 18, 2025. https://www.investopedia.com/how-to-buy-a-car-from-a-dealership-8687310.

Bloomenthal, Andrew. "Credit Card: What It Is, How It Works, and How to Get One." Investopedia. September 30, 2024. https://www.investopedia.com/terms/c/creditcard.asp.

BookRags. "Style in Ithaka." In *Ithaka Study Guide*. Accessed August 9, 2025. https://www.bookrags.com/studyguide-ithaka/style.html.

Bradley, Shannon. "How To Buy a Used Car From a Private Seller." NerdWallet. Updated November 12, 2025. https://www.nerdwallet.com/article/loans/auto-loans/tips-for-buying-a-used-car-from-a-private-seller.

Brady, Ryan. "Liability Car Insurance: What It Covers and How Much You Need." NerdWallet. March 28, 2024. https://www.nerdwallet.com/article/insurance/auto/liability-car-insurance.

Cabello, Marcus. "What Banks Do with Your Money After You Deposit It." Bankrate. June 17, 2025. https://www.bankrate.com/banking/what-banks-do-with-deposits/.

Capital One. "How to Get a Credit Card." February 6, 2025. https://www.capitalone.com/learn-grow/money-management/how-to-apply-for-a-credit-card/.

Chase Bank. "Co-Signing for a Mortgage: What Borrowers and Co-Signers Need to Know." Accessed July 23, 2025. https://www.chase.com/personal/mortgage/education/financing-a-home/cosigning-a-mortgage-loan.

Chase Bank. "Understanding the Costs of Leasing a Car." Chase Auto Education. Accessed August 25, 2025. https://www.chase.com/personal/auto/education/leasing/cost-of-leasing-a-car.

Coleman, Evan. "What Is The Average Credit Card Interest Rate This Week?" Forbes Advisor. August 4, 2025, https://www.forbes.com/advisor/credit-cards/average-credit-card-interest-rate/.

Compass Mortgage. "First-Time Homebuyer FAQ: If I Have a Mortgage, Do I Own My Home?" *Compass Mortgage* (blog). August 31, 2023. https://www.compmort.com/first-time-homebuyer-faq-if-i-have-a-mortgage-do-i-own-my-home/.

Consumer Financial Protection Bureau. "What Is a Credit Report?" Credit Reports and Scores. January 29, 2024. https://www.consumerfinance.gov/ask-cfpb/what-is-a-credit-report-en-309/.

Consumer Financial Protection Bureau. "What Is a FICO Score?" September 3, 2020. https://www.consumerfinance.gov/ask-cfpb/what-is-a-fico-score-en-1883/.

Consumer Reports. "How to Buy a Used Car Safely." *Consumer Reports*, March 19, 2025. https://www.consumerreports.org/cars/used-cars/buying-guide/.

CORT Furniture Outlet. "What Does the Gas Bill Include? Gas Bill 101." *CORT Furniture Outlet* (blog). February 19, 2024. https://blog.cortfurnitureoutlet.com/tips/gas-bill-101/.

Dehan, Andrew. "What Is a Conventional Loan?" Bankrate. July 10, 2025. https://www.bankrate.com/mortgages/what-is-a-conventional-loan.

DeNicola, Louis. "Dealer Fees You Should Know When Buying a Car." Credit Karma. November 8, 2024. https://www.creditkarma.com/auto/i/dealer-fees-buying-car.

Din, Benajmin. "How to Find the Best Travel Insurance." NerdWallet. Updated January 21, 2026. https://www.nerdwallet.com/travel/learn/travel-insurance.

DiTocco, Britney. "The Pros and Cons of Living Without a Car." How to Money. February 4, 2025. https://www.howtomoney.com/no-car-no-problem/.

Dulaney, Lauer & Thomas. "The Impact of Uninsured Motorists." Accessed August 14, 2025. https://www.dulaneylauerthomas.com/library/the-impact-of-uninsured-motorists.cfm.

Epstein, Lita. "Credit Unions vs. Banks: What's the Difference?" Investopedia. November 9, 2024. https://www.investopedia.com/credit-unions-vs-banks-4590218.

Estevez, Eric. "What Is Homeowners Insurance and How Does It Work?" Investopedia. March 5, 2024. https://www.investopedia.com/terms/h/homeowners-insurance.asp.

FBNO. "How to Withdraw Money from Your Bank Account." May 18, 2021. https://www.fnbo.com/insights/2021/personal-finance/how-to-withdraw-money-bank-account.

Federal Communications Commission. "Getting Broadband Q&A." Consumer Guides. January 25, 2024. https://www.fcc.gov/consumers/guides/getting-broadband-qa.

Federal Deposit Insurance Corporation. "Understanding Deposit Insurance." FDIC. Updated April 1, 2024. https://www.fdic.gov/resources/deposit-insurance/understanding-deposit-insurance.

Fernando, Jason. "401(k) Plans: What Are They, How They Work." Investopedia. January 24, 2025. https://www.investopedia.com/terms/1/401kplan.asp.

Fernando, Jason. "The Power of Compound Interest: Calculations and Examples." Investopedia. Updated June 14, 2025. https://www.investopedia.com/terms/c/compoundinterest.asp.

Fernando, Jason. "What Is a Certificate of Deposit (CD) Pros and Cons." Investopedia. June 15, 2025. https://www.investopedia.com/terms/c/certificateofdeposit.asp.

FitzGerald, Jake. "Credit Cards 101: A Beginner's Guide to Understanding and Managing Your Card." Motley Fool Money. April 24, 2025. https://www.fool.com/money/credit-cards/guides-tools/beginners-guide-to-credit-cards/.

Flynn, Kathryn. "Medicare Tax: What Is It and Who Pays It?" Investopedia. January 22, 2024. https://www.investopedia.com/medicare-tax-definition-5115380.

Fontinelle, Amy. "Furlough vs. Layoff." Investopedia. October 22, 2024. https://www.investopedia.com/furlough-vs-layoff-5213743.

Fontinelle, Amy. "How to Get Health Insurance?" Investopedia. February 7, 2023. https://www.investopedia.com/how-to-get-health-insurance-4772855.

Fontinelle, Amy. "What Is a Home Inspection Contingency and Why Is It Important?" Investopedia. June 30, 2024. https://www.investopedia.com/articles/mortgages-real-estate/08/home-inspection.asp.

Gratton, Peter. "What Is the Stock Market and How Does It Work?" Investopedia. May 14, 2025. https://www.investopedia.com/terms/s/stockmarket.asp.

Gula, Drew. "The 5 Best Car Insurance Companies of August 2025." NerdWallet. Accessed August 25, 2025. https://www.nerdwallet.com/best/insurance/car-insurance-new-car.

Gusner, Penny. "How Much Car Insurance Do I Need?" Forbes Advisor. Accessed November 13, 2024. https://www.forbes.com/advisor/car-insurance/how-much-car-insurance-do-you-need/.

Haverstic, Clara. "Financial Illiteracy and Its Impact on Your Wallet." MarketWatch Guides. March 28, 2025. https://www.marketwatch.com/financial-guides/banking/financial-literacy-statistics/.

Hayes, Adam. "Investing in Mutual Funds: What They Are and How They Work." Investopedia. January 30, 2025. https://www.investopedia.com/terms/m/mutualfund.asp.

Hipp, Deb. "What Is a Late Fee?" Credit Karma. Updated November 7, 2025. https://www.creditkarma.com/advice/i/what-is-a-late-fee.

Howard, Pat. "Life Insurance: What It Is, How It Works, and How to Buy a Policy." Investopedia. May 8, 2025. https://www.investopedia.com/terms/l/lifeinsurance.asp.

Huffman, Lee. "What's the Difference Between a Store Card and a Credit Card?" Forbes Advisor. February 26, 2025. https://www.forbes.com/advisor/credit-cards/whats-the-difference-between-a-store-card-and-a-credit-card/.

Hussain, Ali. "How to Buy a Car: A Guide to Your Finances." Investopedia. April 18, 2025. https://www.investopedia.com/how-to-buy-a-car-5119472.

Indeed Editorial Team. "Pros and Cons of Staying for a Long Time with One Employer." Updated December 11, 2025. https://www.indeed.com/career-advice/starting-new-job/staying-long-with-one-employer-pros-cons.

Indeed Employer Content Team. "SMART Goals: An Acronym for Success." Indeed. Last updated July 15, 2025. https://www.indeed.com/hire/c/info/smart-goals.

Investopedia Team. "Closing Costs: What They Are and How Much They Cost." Investopedia. October 7, 2024. https://www.investopedia.com/terms/c/closingcosts.asp.

Investopedia Team. "Down Payment: What It Is and How Much Is Required." Investopedia. August 26, 2024. https://www.investopedia.com/terms/d/down_payment.asp.

Investopedia Team. "How to File Your Tax Return." Investopedia. May 4, 2025. https://www.investopedia.com/ask/answers/051415/what-are-different-ways-i-can-file-my-income-tax-return.asp.

Johnson, Holly. "Which Purchases Should Go on Your Credit Card?" CNET Money. August 4, 2023. https://www.cnet.com/personal-finance/credit-cards/which-purchases-should-go-on-your-credit-card/.

Kagan, Julia. "Check: What It Is, How Bank Checks Work, and How to Write One." Investopedia. May 29, 2024. https://www.investopedia.com/terms/c/check.asp.

Kagan, Julia. "Collision Insurance: What It Is, How It Works." Investopedia. Last modified March 7, 2024. https://www.investopedia.com/terms/c/collision-insurance.asp.

Kagan, Julia. "Definition of Retirement and Tips for How to Save, Plan, and Invest." Investopedia. July 18, 2024. https://www.investopedia.com/terms/r/retirement.asp.

Kagan, Julia. "Deposit: Definition, Meaning, Types, and Example." Investopedia. December 14, 2023. https://www.investopedia.com/terms/d/deposit.asp.

Kagan, Julia. "Direct Deposit: What It Is, How It Works, Benefits & Risks?" Investopedia. March 12, 2024. https://www.investopedia.com/terms/d/directdeposit.asp.

Kagan, Julia. "Health Insurance: Definition, How It Works." Investopedia. Last modified May 29, 2024. https://www.investopedia.com/terms/h/healthinsurance.asp.

Kagan, Julia. "Local Tax: What It Is and Types." Investopedia. June 16, 2024. https://www.investopedia.com/terms/l/localtax.asp.

Kagan, Julia. "Understanding Auto Insurance: Coverage, Costs, and How It Works." Investopedia. Updated November 10, 2025. https://www.investopedia.com/terms/a/auto-insurance.asp.

Kagan, Julia. "Unemployment Insurance (UI): How It Works, Requirements, and Funding." Investopedia. July 8, 2024. https://www.investopedia.com/terms/u/unemployment-insurance.asp.

Kagan, Julia. "What Does Tax Deductible Mean, and What Are Common Deductions?" Investopedia. Updated October 18, 2024. https://www.investopedia.com/terms/d/deductible.asp.

Kagan, Julia. "What Is a Mortgage? Types, How They Work, and Examples." Investopedia. July 19, 2024. https://www.investopedia.com/terms/m/mortgage.asp.

Kagan, Julia. "What Is an Umbrella Insurance Policy? Definition and Who Needs It." Investopedia. Updated January 26, 2024. https://www.investopedia.com/terms/u/umbrella-insurance-policy.asp.

Kagan, Julia. "What Is Comprehensive Insurance and What Does It Cover?" Investopedia. July 19, 2024. https://www.investopedia.com/terms/c/comprehensive-insurance.asp.

Kagan, Julia. "What Is Income Tax and How Are Different Types Calculated?" Investopedia. June 24, 2024. https://www.investopedia.com/terms/i/incometax.asp.

Kagan, Julia. "What Is Insurance?" Investopedia. May 8, 2025. https://www.investopedia.com/terms/i/insurance.asp.

Kenton, Jill. "Subprime Meltdown: What Was It, What Happened, Consequences?" Investopedia. Updated September 10, 2024. https://www.investopedia.com/terms/s/subprime-meltdown.asp.

Koppenheffer, Matt. "Best Credit Cards of August 2025." Motley Fool Money. Accessed August 1, 2025. https://www.fool.com/the-ascent/credit-cards/articles/how-do-credit-cards-work/.

Lee, Matt. "Fixed and Variable Rate Loans: Which Is Better?" Investopedia. July 19, 2024. https://www.investopedia.com/ask/answers/07/fixed-variable.asp.

Lewis, Holden. "Real Estate Agent Commission: How Your Agent Gets Paid." NerdWallet. Updated August 17, 2024. https://www.nerdwallet.com/article/mortgages/real-estate-agent-commission.

Li Cain, Sarah. "Do I Need a Real Estate Agent to Buy a House?" Bankrate. January 11, 2025. https://www.bankrate.com/real-estate/should-i-buy-house-without-realtor/.

Marder, Andrew. "What Is Uninsured Motorist Coverage?" NerdWallet. June 8, 2023. https://www.nerdwallet.com/article/insurance/uninsured-motorist-coverage.

Marshall, Garry, dir. *Pretty Woman.* 1990; Touchstone Pictures.

Messier, Sean. "Checking vs. Savings Accounts: The Difference Explained." Investopedia. May 2, 2025. https://www.investopedia.com/checking-vs-savings-accounts-4783514.

Montoya, Ronald. "Leasing vs. Buying a Car: Which Is Better for You?" Edmunds. December 1, 2020. https://www.edmunds.com/car-leasing/should-you-lease-or-buy-your-car.html.

Myers, Daniel. "Bundle Your Insurance for Big Savings." Investopedia. January 23, 2022. https://www.investopedia.com/articles/insurance/09/bundle-insurance.asp.

National Grid. "What Is Green Energy?" Last updated August 9, 2023. https://www.nationalgrid.com/stories/energy-explained/what-is-green-energy.

New York State Department of Public Service. "Your Rights as a Residential Gas, Electric or Steam Customer Under HEFPA." Consumer Publications. Accessed July 2, 2025. https://dps.ny.gov/consumer-guide-your-rights-residential-gas-electric-or-steam-customer-under-hefpa.

Omojola, Funto. "What Is a Car Warranty?" NerdWallet. Updated November 19, 2025. https://www.nerdwallet.com/article/loans/auto-loans/what-is-a-car-warranty.

Payroll Partners. "Can You Make Direct Deposit Mandatory?" Payroll Partners. Accessed April 10, 2025. https://www.payrollpartners.com/make-direct-deposit-mandatory/.

Peters, Katelyn. "What Is Social Security Tax? Definition, Exemptions, and Example." Investopedia. September 6, 2024. https://www.investopedia.com/terms/s/social-security-tax.asp.

Phillips, Gregory Erich. "Should I Get a Loan Through a Mortgage Company or Bank?" SmartAsset. Updated October 28, 2025. https://smartasset.com/mortgage/should-i-get-my-loan-through-a-mortgage-company-or-a-bank.

Progressive Insurance. "Buying a Car Out of State." Progressive Answers. Accessed August 25, 2025. https://www.progressive.com/answers/buying-a-car-out-of-state/.

PropertyClub Team. "What Is a Utility Bill: Guide and Costs." *PropertyClub* (blog). June 12, 2022. https://propertyclub.nyc/article/what-is-a-utility-bill-guide-and-costs.

Reardon, Kathleen Kelley. *The Skilled Negotiator: Mastering the Language of Engagement.* San Francisco: Jossey-Bass, 2004.

Roberte, Lorraine. "Debt-to-Income (DTI) Ratio: What's Good and How To Calculate It." Investopedia. April 9, 2025. https://www.investopedia.com/terms/d/dti.asp.

Roberte, Lorraine. "What Is Online Banking? Definition and How It Works." Investopedia. February 28, 2025. https://www.investopedia.com/terms/o/onlinebanking.asp.

Rock, Chris. *Bigger and Blacker*, television comedy special. Directed by Keith Truesdell. HBO, July 10, 1999.

Ross, Sean. "Federal Withholding Tax vs. State Withholding Tax: What's the Difference?" Investopedia. November 22, 2024. https://www.investopedia.com/ask/answers/051515/what-difference-between-federal-and-state-withholding-tax.asp.

Ross, Sean. "How Savings Account Interest Rates Are Determined." Investopedia. October 29, 2023. https://www.investopedia.com/ask/answers/043015/what-economic-factors-affect-savings-account-rates.asp.

Rossman, Ted. "Can I Buy a Car with a Credit Card?" Bankrate. February 5, 2025. https://www.bankrate.com/credit-cards/advice/buy-car-with-credit-card/.

Segal, Troy. "Open Loop Card: What It Is, How It Works?" Investopedia. February 25, 2024. https://www.investopedia.com/terms/o/open-loop-card.asp.

Segal, Troy. "The Differences Between a Real Estate Agent, a Broker, and a Realtor." Investopedia. July 1, 2025. https://www.investopedia.com/ask/answers/101314/what-are-differences-among-real-estate-agent-broker-and-realtor.asp.

Shop Solar. "Electric Bill: Definition & Meaning." Accessed July 7, 2025. https://shopsolarkits.com/pages/electric-bill-definition.

Smith, Lisa. "Should I Buy a New or Used Car?" Investopedia. January 6, 2024. https://www.investopedia.com/articles/pf/07/neworusedcar.asp.

Stanger, Tobie. "How to Choose a Home Inspector." *Consumer Reports*, Updated May 8, 2025. https://www.consumerreports.org/home-inspections/how-to-choose-a-home-inspector-a7413938402.

Taylor, Kiara. "How to Endorse a Check." Investopedia. July 2, 2024. https://www.Investopedia.com/how-to-endorse-a-check-5188585.

TransUnion. "Paying the Balance vs. Paying the Minimum on a Credit Card." Debt Management. *TransUnion Blog*. Updated January 15, 2024. https://www.transunion.com/blog/debt-management/credit-card-101-paying-the-balance-vs-paying-the-minimum.

U.S. Department of Energy. "Buying Renewable Electricity." Consumer Savings. Accessed December 19, 2025. https://www.energy.gov/energysaver/buying-renewable-electricity.

U.S. Department of Health and Human Services. "About the Affordable Care Act." Accessed August 14, 2025. https://www.hhs.gov/healthcare/about-the-aca/index.html.

U.S. Department of Housing and Urban Development. "Buying a Home." Helping Americans. Accessed July 23, 2025. https://www.hud.gov/helping-americans/buying-a-home.

U.S. Department of Labor. "State Unemployment Insurance Benefits." Employment & Training Administration. Accessed August 27, 2025. https://oui.doleta.gov/unemploy/uifactsheet.asp.

U.S. Energy Information Administration. "Natural Gas Explained." Energy Explained. Last updated October 10, 2024. https://www.eia.gov/energyexplained/natural-gas/.

Ullrich, Jessica. "How to Buy a Car Online." Investopedia. December 30, 2024. https://www.investopedia.com/how-to-buy-a-car-online-7974497.

Upwork Team. "Contract vs. Full-Time Employment: Key Differences Explained." Upwork Resource Center. August 27, 2024. https://www.upwork.com/resources/full-time-job-vs-contract-work.

Veiga, Alex. "Real Estate Lawsuit Settlement Upends Decadeslong Policies That Helped Set Agent Commissions." AP News, March 15, 2024. https://apnews.com/article/national-association-of-realtors-agent-commissions-lawsuits-d62a66cb80639be3c4c3b429053a22c5.

Well, Libby. "What Is a Good Credit Score to Buy a House?" Bankrate. June 26, 2025. https://www.bankrate.com/real-estate/what-credit-score-do-you-need-to-buy-a-house/.

White, Claire Boyte. "How Is Social Security Tax Calculated?" Investopedia. June 2, 2025. https://www.investopedia.com/ask/answers/081915/how-social-security-tax-calculated.asp.

Zitter, Leah. "Here's How to Get a Car with No Down Payment." Investopedia. April 7, 2023. https://www.investopedia.com/articles/company-insights/083016/heres-how-get-car-no-down-payment.asp.

ACKNOWLEDGMENTS

I would like to express my deepest gratitude to Dr. Michael King, who took the time to listen to my many conversations about the importance of personal financial knowledge in our educational system. His insights as a subject matter expert—and his thoughtful advice—helped shape how I approached this project.

To Thomas F. Monteleone, who gave me one of the most valuable pieces of advice I've ever received: "Don't talk about it—write about it." Those words became a guiding principle throughout this journey.

To Tsafrir Oranski, who read early drafts of this book during long flights and found humor and connection in its pages. Your encouragement and laughter reminded me why these stories matter.

To Mark Cohen, who believed in this project from the very first time I shared the idea. Your steady encouragement kept me going.

To Jessie Rothkuo, whose ongoing support—both for this book and for my work with the children of Little Flower—means more than words can express.

To the entire team at Luminare Press, who served as my blueprint and compass in the publishing world. You taught me lessons about this process that are truly priceless. Your guidance, patience, and professionalism turned a complex journey into a rewarding experience.

To my illustrator, Eshan Sulakkana, whose creative brilliance brought my ideas to life. Every illustration in this book reflects your dedication and artistry. You worked tirelessly, contributed fresh ideas, and never stopped until we got it right.

And finally, to my wife, Zenaye, who understood why writing this book was so important to me. Your patience, love, and shared commitment to helping others avoid becoming victims of financial inexperience have been my greatest motivation and joy.

ABOUT THE AUTHOR

Salzman Epstein Tarver is a university-educated, self-taught financial literacy advocate who has lived, worked, and traveled in over fifteen countries. He learned to manage money through real-life experiences, personal research, and disciplined planning. His journey includes relocating to London and returning to New York City—both times without a job—and navigating uncertainty with smart financial choices and resilience.

Recognizing how many people are left to figure out money matters on their own, Salzman wrote *Your Blueprint for Financial Literacy* to provide clear, relatable guidance on everything from banking and budgeting to credit, insurance, retirement, buying a home, and dealing with unemployment. His mission is to empower readers of all ages to take charge of their financial futures—no finance degree required.